MASTERS OF MUSIC

BEETHOVEN

AND THE CLASSICAL AGE

TEXT
ANDREA BERGAMINI
ILLUSTRATIONS
STUDIO L.R. GALANTE: MANUELA CAPPON, L.R. GALANTE,
ALESSANDRO MENCHI, FRANCESCO SPADONI

DoGi

English translation
© Copyright 1999
by Barron's Educational
Series, Inc.
Original edition © 1998 by
DoGi spa Florence Italy
Title of original edition:
Beethoven e l'età classica
Italian edition by
Andrea Bergamini
Consultant:
Sefano Catucci
Graphic Display and
Illustrations by
Studio L.R. Galante,
Manuela Cappon,
L.R. Galante,
Allessandro Menchi,
Francesco Spadoni
Art director:
Sebastiano Ranchetti
Page make-up:
Sebastiano Ranchetti
Andrea Bachini
Iconographic researcher:
Katherine Carson Forden
Editorial Staff:
Andrea Bachini

English translation by
Venetia Scalo

HOW TO READ THIS BOOK

Each double page constitutes a chapter regarding the life and musical art of Beethoven, great feats in the musical culture of his time, or a detailed analysis of the instruments and/or music theory. The top of the left page (1) and the large central illus-tration refer to the principal theme. The text in italics (2) narrates the life of Beethoven in chronological order. The other elements on the page—photographs, printed reproductions of the era, portraits—complete the treatment of the discussion.

ACKNOWLEDGMENTS

ABBREVIATIONS:
t for **top**, **b** for **below**, **c** for **center**, **r** for **right**, and **l** for **left**.
A particular thank you to Friedhelm Loesti of the Beethoven Haus of Bonn, to Doctor Christoph Ludwig, librarian at the Historical Institute of the Austian Institute of Culture in Rome; and finally to the Deutsche Oper Berlin that has furnished us with the neces-sary documentation to produce the tables on *Fidelio*.
ILLUSTRATIONS:
The illustrations contained in this volume, unedited and original, have been obtained under the auspices and care of DoGi spa, who holds the copyright.
Production: Studio L.R. Galante: Manuela Cappon, L.R. Galante, Alessandro Menchi, Francesco Spadoni
Manuela Cappon: 6–7, 8–9, 10–11, 14–15, 20–21, 38–39, 42–43, 46–47, 54–55, 58–59; Alessandro Menchi: 16–17, 22–23, 26–27, 28–29, 32–33, 40–41, 44–45, 52–53, 56–57; Francesco Spadoni: 4–5, 12–13, 18–19, 24–25, 30–31, 34–35, 36–37, 48–49, 50–51, 60–61.
Computer Elaboration: Luca Cascioli (15, map)
COVER: Alessandro Menchi
FRONTISPIECE: Alessandro Menchi

LIST OF REPRODUCTIONS:
DoGi spa has made every effort to trace all third-party rights. We apologize for any omissions or errors and will be happy to make any corrections in all future editions of this work.
(The works that have been reproduced in their totality are followed by the letter **t**; those that have been reproduced in part are followed by the letter **p**.)
6 Delacroix, Eugène, *Liberty Leading the People*, 1830, oil on canvas, 102 × 120 in (260 × 325 cm) (LOUVRE, PARIS) p; **7l** Anonymous, *The Dance of the Peasant Woman*, print (NATIONAL LIBRARY, PARIS) p; **7r** Anonymous, *Maximilien Robespierre* (CARNAVALET MUSEUM, PARIS) p; **8l** Anonymous, *Maximilian Franz, Elector and Archbishop*, copy in oil of the original in the Brühl Castle (BEETHOVEN HAUS, BONN) p; **9l** *University of Bonn* (PHOTO MICHAEL SONDERMANN; PRESSEAMT BUNDESSTADT BONN) t; **9r** L. Radoux, *Ludwig van Beethoven (Grandfather of the Maestro)*, oil painting (OTTO REICHERT, VIENNA) p; **10l** Anonymous, *W. A. Mozart* (GESELLSCHAFT DER MUSIKFREUNDE, VIENNA) p; **10r** Frontispiece of the original edition of Beethoven's *Three Sonatas op. 2* (HISTORISCHES MUSEUM DER STADT, VIENNA) t; **12** Daniel Huber, Map of Vienna, 1785, engraving (HISTORISCHES MUSEUM DER STADT, VIENNA) t; **14** F. Pfeiffer, *Prince Franz Joseph Max Lobkowitz*, engraving (AUSTRIAN NATIONAL LIBRARY, VIENNA) p; **16** E. Smith, *Snuffbox*, 1855, silver, with engraved decora-tion, t; **17** C. F. Riedel, *Abbot Joseph Gelinek*, engraving (BEETHOVEN HAUS, BONN) t; **18t** Score of the first of twelve symphonies writ-ten by Dittersdorf based on a cycle of episodes taken from Ovid's *Metamorphoses* (GESELLSCHAFT DER MUSIKFREUNDE, VIENNA) t; **18b** Page from the score of *The Fairy Queen* by Henry Purcell (ROYAL COLLEGE OF MUSIC, LONDON) t; **20** Playbill of *Quintet in E Flat Major op. 16* by Beethoven, April 6, 1797 (GESELLSCHAFT DER MUSIKFREUNDE, VIENNA) t; **21** *Piano Concerto No. 4 op. 58*, 1808 (GESELLSCHAFT DER MUSIKFREUNDE, VIENNA) t; **22l** Caspar David Friedrich, *Wanderer Above the Sea of Fog*, 1818, oil on canvas (IGDA, MILAN) p; **22r** Anonymous, *The Magic Lantern*, circa 1870, engraving (MARY EVANS PICTURE LIBRARY, LONDON) t; **23** Hanfstängl from a painting by J. Stieler, *Friedrich Schelling*, lithograph (HISTORISCHES MUSEUM DER STADT, VIENNA) t; **24** Edward Scriven, *Muzio Clementi*, engraving (IGDA, MILAN) p; **25** Original edition of *Symphony No. 3 in E Flat Major op. 55 "Symphony Eroica"* (GESELLSCHAFT DER MUSIKFREUNDE, VIENNA) t; **26** Deluxe binding of the *Piano Sonata in D Major op. 28* by Beethoven (BEETHOVEN HAUS, BONN) t; **27** *From a pocket notebook*, 1818 (GESELLSCHAFT DER MUSIKFREUNDE, VIENNA) t; **29** *The Heiligenstadt Testament*, October 6, 1802 (STATE UNIVERSITY LIBRARY, HAMBURG) p; **30l** Anonymous, *Karl van Beethoven*, circa 1825, miniature (HISTORISCHES MUSEUM DER STADT, VIENNA) t; **30r** Frontispiece of the original edition of *Wellington's Victory* for piano two hands (BEETHOVEN ARCHIVES, BONN) t; **32** Alois Karner, *Sonnleithner*, 1820, platinotype (HISTORISCHES MUSEUM DER STADT, VIENNA) t; **33** Scenes from Cherubini's opera *Medea* with Maria Callas, 1953–54 (ARCHIVIO FOTOGRAFICO TEATRO ALLA SCALA, MILAN) p; **34** Anonymous, *Antonia von Brentano*, circa 1800 (PRIVATE COLLECTION) t; **36** Herbert von Karajan (RCS-IGDA, MILAN) p; **37** August Borckmann, *Beethoven Conducting the Rasoumovsky Quartet* (BEETHOVEN HAUS, BONN) p; **38l** Anonymous, *Clemens Brentano*, engraving (MARY EVANS PICTURE LIBRARY, LONDON) t; **38r** *The Entrance of Hans Sachs*, Act III, Scene ii from Goethe's opera *The Master Singers*, 1993 (DEUTSCHE OPER, BERLIN; KRANICHPHOTO, BERLIN) t; **39** William Nicholson, *George Thompson*, circa 1816, watercolor drawing (SCOTTISH NATIONAL PORTRAIT GALLERY, EDINBURGH) t; **40** Daniel Chodowiecki, cover of *The Sorrows of Young Werther*, 1778 edition, engraving (MARY EVANS PICTURE LIBRARY, LONDON) t; **41** Anonymous, *An Ear*, circa 1880, color engraving from *The Normal Life* (MARY EVANS PICTURE LIBRARY, LONDON) p; **42** Anonymous, Scene from Goethe's opera *Egmont*, engraving (RCS, MILAN) p; **43** Scene from the Stanley Kubrick film *A Clockwork Orange*, 1971 (WARNER BROS; THE KOBAL COLLECTION, LONDON) t; **44** Le Campion, *Pilatre de Rozier and the Marquis d'Arlandes Make the First Successful Flight in a Hot-Air Balloon in Paris*, 1783, from *L'Histoire de l'Aéronautique* (MARY EVANS PICTURE LIBRARY, LONDON) t; **45** Anonymous, *A Session of the Congress of Vienna*, popular print of the epoch (DoGi ARCHIVE, FLORENCE) t; **46** Gause, *Franz Joseph at a Vienna Ball*, 1900 (DoGi ARCHIVE, FLORENCE) p; **47** Anonymous, *Johann Strauss Jr.*, painting (IGDA, MILAN) p; **48l** G. B. Lampi, *Andreas Kyrillowitz Rasoumovsky*, oil painting (HISTORISCHES MUSEUM DER STADT, VIENNA) p; **48c** Anonymous, *The Fourfold Music Stand*, nineteenth century (BUNDESSAMMLUNG ALTER STILMÖBEL, VIENNA) t; **50l** Vincenzo Camuccini, *Gioacchino Rossini*, painting (MUSEO TEATRALE ALLA SCALA, MILAN) p; **50r** Frontispiece of the original edition of the *Missa Solemnis in D Major op. 123*, 1827 (BEETHOVEN ARCHIVE, BONN) t; **51** *Queen of the Night* from W. A. Mozart's *The Magic Flute*, opening of the 1995–96 season, La Scala Theater, Milan (FOTO LELLI & MASOTTI/ARCHIVIO FOTOGRAFICO TEATRO ALLA SCALA, MILAN) p; **54t** *Schwarzspanierhaus*, Vienna (IGDA, MILAN) t; **54b** *Gravy Boat*, Empire style, Brussels, 1820 (IGDA, MILAN) t; **55** *A Page from Beethoven's Conversation Notebooks* (H. C. BODMER COLLECTION/ BEETHOVEN HAUS, BONN) t; **56** Anonymous, *Austrian Policeman*, lithograph, circa 1820–25 (HISTORISCHES MUSEUM DER STADT, VIENNA) p; **57** Frontispiece of the score of the original edition of the *Ninth Symphony in D Minor op. 125*, 1826 (BEETHOVEN ARCHIVE, BONN) t; **58t** Wilhelm August Rieder, *Franz Schubert*, 1825, watercolor (HISTORISCHES MUSEUM DER STADT, VIENNA) p; **58b** E. Kaiser, *Clara and Robert Schumann*, drawing (IGDA, MILAN) p; **59t** Caroline Bardua, *Carl Maria von Weber*, oil on canvas (AKG, BERLIN) p; **59b** Wilhelm Hensel, *Jacob Felix Mendelssohn Bartholdy*, 1829, watercolor (LEBRECHT COLLECTION) p; **60** Joseph Kriehuber, *Anton Diabelli*, litho-graph (NATIONALBIBLIOTHEK, VIENNA) p; **60c** Igor Stravinsky (FOTO ERICH AUERBACH) p; **61** *Invitation to Beethoven's Funeral*, March 1827 (BEETHOVEN HAUS, BONN) t

COVER (CLOCKWISE FROM TOP LEFT)
1. W. J. Mähler, *Ludwig van Beethoven*, 1815, oil painting (GESELLSCHAFT DER MUSIKFREUNDE, VIENNA) p; **2.** 45 t; **3.** L. Janscha, *Mödling's Throat*, watercolor (ALBERTINA COLLECTION, VIENNA) p; **4.** J. B. Lampi the Elder, *Countess Teresa von Brunswick*, copy in oil (BEETHOVEN HAUS, BONN) p; **5.** 7l; **6.** 34 t; **7.** 18t t; **8.** 22l p; **9.** 7r p; **10.** 51 p; **11.** *Illustration of Act I, Scene IV of Fidelio*, circa 1885, lithograph (LIEBIG POSTCARD COLLECTION) p; **12.** 9r p; **13.** 46 p
BACK COVER:
W. J. Mähler, *Ludwig van Beethoven*, circa 1804, oil painting (HISTORISCHES MUSEUM DER STADT, VIENNA) p

CONTENTS

THE PROTAGONISTS

Between 1700 and 1800, in the Europe of Napoleon and Metternich, a restless and talented musician lived. Agile and powerful at the piano, he gained immense fame as a composer. His name was Ludwig van Beethoven (1770–1827) and he had no doubt about the greatness of his own music. In Vienna, the aristocracy supported him financially, and the major European publishers paid a great deal of money for the privilege of publishing his works. Beethoven was therefore free of the humiliating obligations of a court assignment and could dedicate himself completely to his own genius. A student of Haydn, from whom he learned the rules of the classical style of music, he reformed its principles very early on, and the novelty of his departures astonished everyone.

◆ **HIS GRAND-FATHER, HIS FATHER, AND HIS MOTHER** Ludwig van Beethoven (1712–1773) was the paternal grand-father, a choirmaster in Bonn and a wine merchant.

Johann (1740–1792), father of Ludwig, also a court musician in Bonn, married Maria Magdalena (1746–1787) in 1768, daughter of the inspector of the court kitchens at Treviri.

◆ **SCHUPPANZIGH IGNAZ** (1776–1830) Violinist, true friend of Beethoven, and careful performer of his music.

◆ **SISTER-IN-LAW AND NEPHEW** Wife of his brother Caspar Carl, she was dragged to court by Beethoven, over the guardianship of her son Karl.

◆ **THE PUBLISHERS** Artaria & Co. was founded in 1778 in Vienna by the brothers Cesare, Domenico, and Giovanni Artaria. After having estab-lished itself as one of the most impor-tant publishing houses in Europe, it acquired even more prestige by publishing many of Beethoven's works.

◆ **GOETHE** (1749–1832) Novelist, playwright, poet, and philosopher, he was the most important German intellectual of the age.

◆ **HAYDN** (1732–1809) Composer of European fame and, along with Mozart, father of Viennese classicism.

◆ **SCHUBERT AND ROSSINI** Among the most appreciated composers of the epoch, both were great admir-ers of Beethoven.

♦ **THE IMMORTAL BELOVED**
Recipient of a famous love letter by Ludwig van Beethoven. Despite the indiscreet curiosity of many scholars, she still hid her face.

♦ **THE PATRONS**
Princes Lichnowsky and Lobkowitz and Archduke Rudolph were among Beethoven's principal patrons. They understood art and supported it generously.

♦ **MAXIMILIAN FRANZ**
Principal elector at Bonn in 1784, he introduced the typical reforms of so-called enlightened despotism to the small principality.

♦ **BEETHOVEN**
(1770–1827)
Robust and short of stature, with raven hair and an olive complexion, he was striking primarily for the intensity of his gaze.

♦ **SCHINDLER**
(1798–1864)
After having abandoned his studies to dedicate himself to music, he met Beethoven in 1814, and became his faithful secretary.

♦ **ROBESPIERRE**
(1758–1794)
Protagonist in the Revolution that, beginning in 1789, upset France. His name was linked mainly with the Reign of Terror.

♦ **METTERNICH AND NAPOLEON**
Metternich was Austrian Chancellor from 1809 until the Revolution of 1848; Napoleon was controller of European political and military life from 1796 to 1815.

THE IDEALS OF 1789

With the French Revolution, which began in 1789, the order that had dominated Europe for centuries, the so-called Ancient Regime, collapsed. The king's absolute power over the state, the privileges of the nobility and the high clergy, the exclusive access reserved for the aristocrats to the highest levels of public administration, the army, and the magistracy, were by now already in a long-time conflict with the interests of a bourgeoisie that had developed its own manufacturing and commercial activities and that demanded economic freedom, lower taxes, and more political power. With the Revolution, all citizens became equal under the law and had the right to express their own ideas. An incredulous Europe learned that even kings may be beheaded and that the republic—a state governed by all its citizens—was not a utopia but a reality.

♦ THE MOST WIDESPREAD SONGS

During the years of the Revolution, the song was the most widespread musical genre since it lent itself to the development of the political and educational task that the ruling republican class expected from the arts. The texts of the songs exalted civic virtues, universal principles, and the events and heroes of the Revolution. For music, one returned most often to arias that were familiar and simple so that their impact would be greater and their distribution easier. The songs were born spontaneously in the most diverse settings. Composers of songs were, in fact, farmers or workers or artisans. Among the most celebrated of these songs were *The Taking of the Bastille* and above all *The Marseillaise.* Composed in 1792 by Claude Rouget de Lisle for the proclamation of the war in Austria, it became the national anthem on July 14, 1795. Above, Eugène Delacroix, *Liberty Leading the People,* Louvre; detail.

♦ THE FESTIVAL OF THE SUPREME BEING

The Festival of the Supreme Being was celebrated on June 20, 1794. A symbolic mountain, on which the deputies of the Convention and a few chorus members took their place, was raised on the parade ground. The spectacle included a performance for the populace of a few verses by Marie Joseph Chenier to the melody of *The Marseillaise.*

♦ THE TREE OF LIBERTY

It was planted in all the French squares to symbolize the freedom won by the Revolution of 1789.

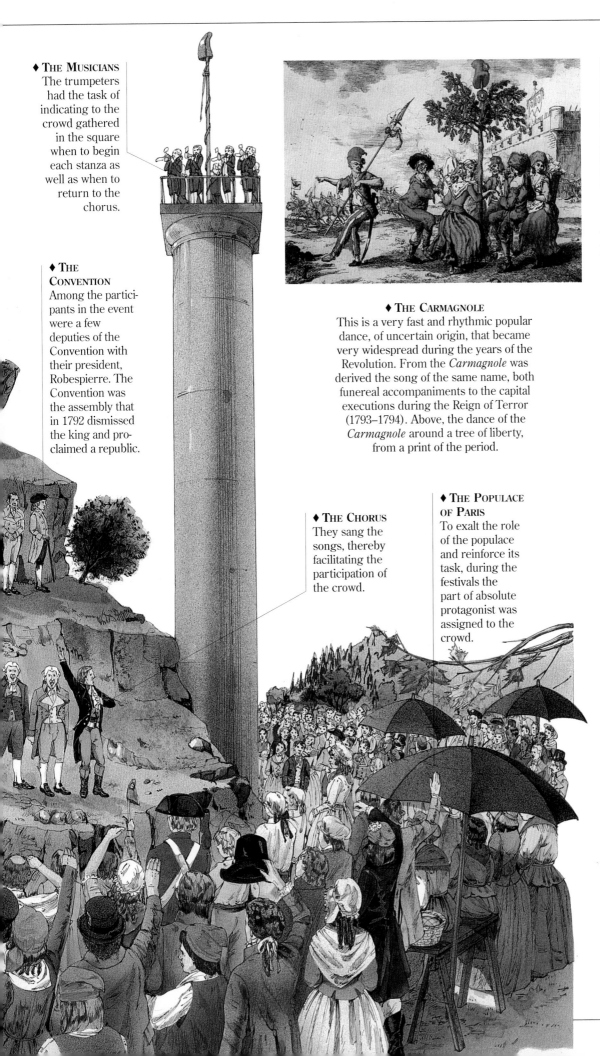

♦ **THE MUSICIANS**
The trumpeters had the task of indicating to the crowd gathered in the square when to begin each stanza as well as when to return to the chorus.

♦ **THE CONVENTION**
Among the participants in the event were a few deputies of the Convention with their president, Robespierre. The Convention was the assembly that in 1792 dismissed the king and proclaimed a republic.

♦ **THE CARMAGNOLE**
This is a very fast and rhythmic popular dance, of uncertain origin, that became very widespread during the years of the Revolution. From the *Carmagnole* was derived the song of the same name, both funereal accompaniments to the capital executions during the Reign of Terror (1793–1794). Above, the dance of the *Carmagnole* around a tree of liberty, from a print of the period.

♦ **THE CHORUS**
They sang the songs, thereby facilitating the participation of the crowd.

♦ **THE POPULACE OF PARIS**
To exalt the role of the populace and reinforce its task, during the festivals the part of absolute protagonist was assigned to the crowd.

♦ **THE CULT OF THE REVOLUTION**
With the 1789 privileges of the nobility abolished and the power of the king limited, in 1792 the bourgeoisie overthrew the monarchy and proclaimed the republic. In 1793, the Committee of Public Health, instituted to protect the Revolution from external and internal threats, suppressed all contrary voices: these were the years of the Reign of Terror (1793–1794). Maximilien Robespierre (above) emerged from the Committee, who added to the repression the search for a consensus regarding the gains of the Revolution. With this strategy, the cult of the Supreme Being was reborn, and instituted by Robespierre to give a sacred foundation to civic virtues and to absorb the need for religious devotion, so widespread among the populace. The celebration of the cult was assigned to a festival where grandiose sets and solemn music reinforced, among the masses, solidarity toward the government.

BONN

Situated to the east of the Rhine and near the French border, Bonn was the residence of the court of the Electoral Archbishop of Cologne, one of the most important principalities that form Germany. Officially, this principality was unified under the German Empire; in reality it was divided into a myriad of sovereign states. Thanks to the action of the Prince Archbishop Maximilian Franz (ruler from 1784–1794), Bonn was one of the most advanced centers of "enlightened despotism," an expression that defined the pledge of some European sovereigns, at the end of the 1700s, to modernize the state with public works and cultural and assistance initiatives, without limiting their own absolute power.

♦ THE PRINCE ARCHBISHOP

The year 1784 saw the rise to the rank of Archbishop of Cologne of Maximilian Franz (1756–1801)—in the portrait above—brother of Emperor Joseph II. Lover of the good life and passionate about music, he promoted the spirit of reform of the European Enlightenment in the small principality. Moreover, he established a commission that oversaw the reform of the judicial system, abolished torture, curtailed the privileges of the nobility, and opened a room for public reading in the palace's library. The actions of Maximilian Franz stimulated the cultural ambiance of Bonn, where there emerged a group of progressive intellectuals, gathered around the Zehrgartner, a tavern with an antique bookstore; here Beethoven had his first cultural formation, nourished by his readings of Goethe and Schiller.

♦ THE CHORUS

During the performance of a liturgical chant, Beethoven improvised a rich and difficult accompaniment that confused the members of the chorus. Some of them personally complained to Maximilian Franz.

♦ THE YOUNG BEETHOVEN

In 1784, the young Beethoven was appointed organist, a position that paid a regular annual salary of 150 florins. Occasionally he even substituted for Maestro Neefe at the cymbals in the orchestra of the court theater.

♦ THE MAESTRO

Validating and disciplining the talent of the young Beethoven was Gottlob Neefe, from 1881 organist at the court of Bonn, and a highly cultured and trained musician.

♦ THE FATHER

Mediocre violinist and choir member at the court of Bonn. Often inebriated, his presence in the chorus gallery was barely tolerated. Sometimes violent, he forced the small Ludwig to practice for hours at the violin and piano.

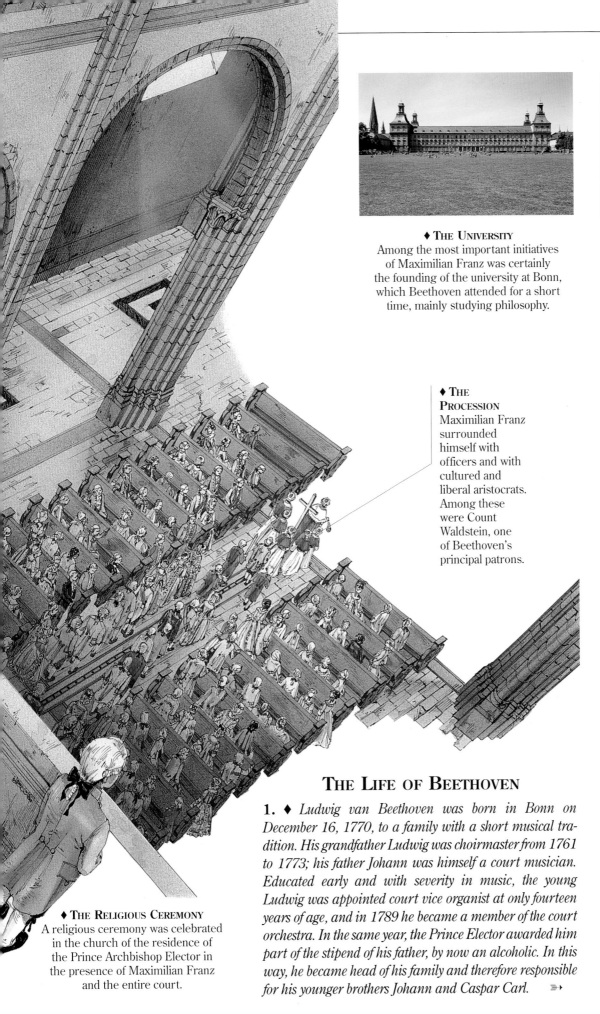

♦ **THE UNIVERSITY**
Among the most important initiatives of Maximilian Franz was certainly the founding of the university at Bonn, which Beethoven attended for a short time, mainly studying philosophy.

♦ **THE SERVANT MUSICIAN**
Economic autonomy, and consequently creative autonomy, was something not yet attained by German musicians. Beethoven would make an important contribution in this field, but only after moving to Vienna. At Bonn, Beethoven was still a part of the system that regulated the musical life of much of the German world. This system was that of the court that, because of its own needs for entertainment or celebration, endowed itself with an orchestral group, regularly salaried and without any creative autonomy. The person responsible for the musical life of the court was the choirmaster. He composed Masses, operas, symphonies, and dances, according to the needs of the court. He was also responsible for keeping the instruments in good condition and for the discipline of his musicians. Above, Beethoven's grandfather.

♦ **THE PROCESSION**
Maximilian Franz surrounded himself with officers and with cultured and liberal aristocrats. Among these were Count Waldstein, one of Beethoven's principal patrons.

♦ **THE RELIGIOUS CEREMONY**
A religious ceremony was celebrated in the church of the residence of the Prince Archbishop Elector in the presence of Maximilian Franz and the entire court.

THE LIFE OF BEETHOVEN

1. ♦ *Ludwig van Beethoven was born in Bonn on December 16, 1770, to a family with a short musical tradition. His grandfather Ludwig was choirmaster from 1761 to 1773; his father Johann was himself a court musician. Educated early and with severity in music, the young Ludwig was appointed court vice organist at only fourteen years of age, and in 1789 he became a member of the court orchestra. In the same year, the Prince Elector awarded him part of the stipend of his father, by now an alcoholic. In this way, he became head of his family and therefore responsible for his younger brothers Johann and Caspar Carl.* ≫‣

THE CLASSICAL STYLE

In the Vienna of the late 1700s a new musical style, classicism, had already affirmed itself. It is a language that addresses, above all, instrumental music—the symphony and the string quartet in particular. The fathers of the classical style were Mozart and Haydn. The latter, from 1791 to 1795, composed, for two seasons of public concerts in London, twelve symphonies that revealed the principal character of Viennese classicism: a great richness of rhythms, sounds, and accompaniment, inserted and organized into a solid and well-thought-out structure made up of perfect symmetries and rigorous proportions among its diverse components.

♦ **FORMS AND STRUCTURE OF CLASSICISM**
The classical style seeks to enrich musical pieces and give them coherence. The structure of a classical work calls for, in general, four movements, consisting of the placement of one slow tempo among three lively ones. The initial allegro is constructed according to a composition outline called sonata-form. This subdivides the movement into three different sections: exposition, development, and recapitulation. Two themes are presented in the exposition, joined by harmonic relationships and constructed according to rigid symmetries between their parts. In the development, the thematic material is subject to elaboration; it is therefore modified and embellished in some of its aspects. In the recapitulation the themes of the exposition are presented in the original key, thus giving unity to the movement. Above, a portrait of Mozart.

♦ **BEETHOVEN AND HAYDN**
Between 1792 and 1794 Haydn gave Beethoven composition lessons that were a bit distracted. (Above, frontispiece of the *Three Sonatas Op. 2* dedicated to Haydn.)

♦ **HAYDN**
With masks, he illustrated the characters of the four movements of the new symphony, pride of the Viennese classical style.

♦ **SALOMON**
Violinist and composer, he was famous primarily for his activities as impresario, which he developed in London from 1781. A friend of Haydn, he convinced him in 1790 to compose a cycle of twelve symphonies for two seasons of public concerts in London.

♦ **THE PRESENTATION OF THE GRACES**
In a public concert at the Hanover Square rooms of London, Haydn had himself accompanied by four pleasant masked women, which he presented as his Graces.

2. THE LIFE OF BEETHOVEN ♦ *Between 1789 and 1792 Beethoven was already a protagonist in the musical life of Bonn, esteemed by the Prince Elector as well as by some of the most eminent personalities of the city. The life of the young musician witnessed a decisive turn in 1792, when Haydn, upon returning from London, accepted hospitality at the court of Bonn. Count Waldstein placed before the Austrian composer one of Beethoven's works, receiving a positive judgment and the promise to accept the young Ludwig as a student. On November 3, 1792, Beethoven left for Vienna.* ➤

♦ **L'ALLEGRO**
The first grace is spirited and exhuberant, like the final allegro of the symphony.

♦ **L'ADAGIO**
The second grace has the introspective and romantic character of the adagio.

♦ **THE MINUET**
The third grace
is dancing and
carnivalesque,
exactly like
the minuet.

♦ **THE FINAL
ALLEGRO**
The fourth grace
has the noble and
classic character of
the initial allegro.

THE CITY OF MUSIC

The Vienna that welcomed Beethoven was the capital of the vast Austrian Empire, but it was also an extraordinary and rather intricate musical center. Three ideal personages will help us travel through it: the aristocrat, the bourgeois, and the commoner. The aristrocrat listened to excellent music in the palaces of the most well-known nobility and frequented mostly the imperial theaters, where he could attend the cultured Italian *opera seria*. The bourgeois, promoter of public concerts, preferred the vivacity of works from the suburbs to the pretentious imperial ones. The commoner, finally, delighted himself at inns with street musicians and stood in line at the suburban theaters for the more spectacular and vulgar *singspiel*.

♦ **VIENNA IN 1785**
Toward the end of the eighteenth century, the Austrian capital consisted of 247,000 inhabitants.

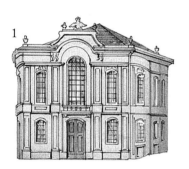

♦ **COURT THEATERS**
The Burgtheater (1) was founded by Maria Theresa in 1741 and was transformed into a national theater by Joseph II in 1776, with the intention of promoting German opera and drama. The Kärntnerthor (2) was the principal court theater, with a professional orchestra and a rich program of *opera seria,* mainly Italian. Subsidized by the state and managed by a council of aristocrats, the court theaters combined budget requirements with high-quality musical offerings.

♦ **PALACES OF THE BOURGEOISIE**
From the first years of the 1800s, members of the Viennese bourgeoisie, in particular the financial one, organized important musical evenings in their own homes.

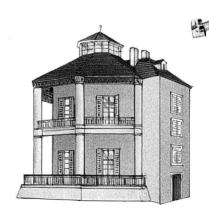

♦ **THE INNS**
Preferred by street musicians, sometimes they hosted cultured music also, such as the Wilden Zum Mann (at left) with Beethoven's *Quartet Op. 132.*

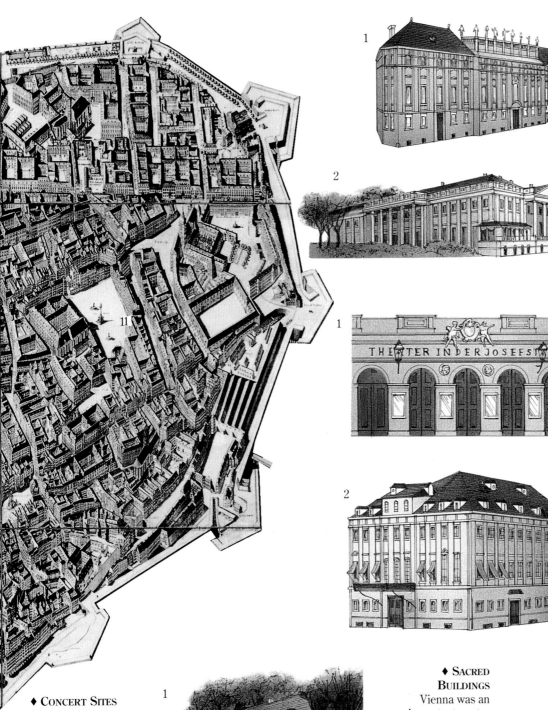

♦ **THE PALACES OF THE ARISTOCRACY**
Lobkowitz Palace (1) and Rasoumovsky Palace (2). Orchestral groups but more often chamber bands were at the service of princes and counts: the nobility could, in this way, listen to music of the highest level in their own palaces.

♦ **THE SUBURBAN THEATERS**
The Josefstadt Theater (1) and the Theater an der Wien (2) were private theaters that, in order to balance their accounts, staged productions that were decidedly more popular than those staged in court theaters. These gave preference to the *opera buffa,* the *singspiel,* and the *opera comique.* They often offered public concerts and charged admission.

♦ **CONCERT SITES**
Concerts were held in theaters or in other places temporarily designated for this purpose. The most important were the Pavillion of Augartner (1), where concert series were organized that were open to all citizens, and the Redoutensaal (2), normally a ball-room for the imperial court.

♦ **SACRED BUILDINGS**
Vienna was an important center for the production of sacred music. The Catholic church promoted the composition of new music to be performed mainly in the Cathedral of Saint Stephen. An analogous activity was also developed by the Hebrew community, in whose synagogue could be heard modern sacred music.

THE PATRONS

Animating the musical Vienna at the end of the century was mainly the cultured aristocracy that, almost every night during the winter season, hosted in their own palaces musical encounters with high-level instrumentalists. The aristocracy spent a great deal of money maintaining chamber music bands or supporting young musicians, somewhat in return for entertainment, but in truth more for prestige. The dedication of a valued composer or the protection of a famous musician assured the patron of appreciation by high society. Sensitive to the values of art, the Viennese aristocracy had the unquestioned honor of having promoted the creativity of many musicians, freeing them of the tedious obligations of court employment.

♦ PRINCE LOBKOWITZ
Franz Joseph Maximilian Lobkowitz (1772–1816)—above—belonged to a Bohemian family with a long tradition of artistic and musical patronage. A fairly good musician, he promoted musical initiatives first in Prague and then in Vienna. He was one of Beethoven's most generous patrons, whom at first he supported by acquiring works and later actually awarding him a salary (in 1809) through a contract that was most advantageous for the musician.

♦ THE CONCERT HALL
In 1804, it was the theater of the historic first performance of one of Beethoven's most important symphonies, number 3, entitled *Eroica*.

♦ THE GUESTS
The musical evenings in the palaces of the aristocracy were certainly exclusive but not closed to the more well-known members of the bourgeoisie.

♦ WALKING MUSICIANS
Violinists, or even harpists, offering pleasant rhythms and a rich repertoire of popular music.

◆ **Lobkowitz Palace**
Erected between 1685 and 1687.

In 1753 it was acquired by the Lobkowitz family.

◆ **The Empire**
In Vienna, the cosmopolitan aristocracy gathered the dominions of the House of Austria (dark yellow), which extended from the low countries (until 1794) to northern Italy and Dalmatia (from 1799), from Tyrol to Transylvania.

DENMARK

UNITED PROVINCES

POMERANIA · Kaliningrad

BRANDENBURG · PRUSSIA

POLAND

RAVENSBERG

AUSTRIAN LOW COUNTRIES · Cologne · Berlin

SAXONY

Dreseda · Warsaw

Mainz

LOWER PALATINATE · Prague · SILESIA

UPPER PALATINATE · BOHEMIA

FRANCE

BAVARIA · MORAVIA

Salzburg · Vienna

SWITZERLAND · TYROL · STYRIA · Buda Pest

CARINTHIA · HUNGARY TRANSYLVANIA

Trent · CARNIOLA

Milan · **REPUBLIC OF VENICE**

TUSCANY

OTTOMAN EMPIRE

◆ **A Musical Evening**
In the palace of Prince Lobkowitz an important musical evening was about to unfold. In terms of variety and quality, the music performed in private Viennese homes was superior to that of all other European capitals.

◆ **The Orchestra Members**
Prince Lobkowitz was among the few in Vienna to possess a personal orchestra, albeit with a reduced staff.

3. The Life of Beethoven ◆ *In Vienna, after making a few temporary arrangements, Beethoven settled himself in the house of Prince Licknowsky and his wife, Christine. As promised, Haydn began to give him lessons in composition, but the scarce attention of the maestro irritated Beethoven, who secretly turned to another teacher. From 1794, Beethoven increased his composition practice of the counterpoint by studying with Albrechtsbeger, choirmaster at Saint Stephen.* ➠▸

Debuts in Vienna

In Vienna, Beethoven witnessed his first successes thanks to his piano virtuosity, of which he gave ample demonstration in the competitions that were organized in the private salons of the better-known aristocracy. The young Beethoven astounded primarily because of his incredible talent for improvising: he was able, in fact, to embellish with stupefying imagination and rigor a theme he had heard only once. The admiration of his patrons, his growing fame, and even his conspicuous earnings did not divert Beethoven from his iron will to become a composer, to dedicate himself above all to musical creation.

♦ **THE SNUFFBOX**
Whether employed at court or by a gentleman, musicians were thanked for their performance with the gift of a snuffbox. This, then, became the symbol of the servant musician.

♦ **CHRISTINE**
Wife of Prince Carl Lichnowsky, she was an admired pianist who doted on the young Beethoven, lavishing almost excessive care and attention on him.

♦ **LOBKOWITZ AND VON BROWNE-CAMUS**
Prince Lobkowitz converses with Count Browne-Camus, a Russian official in Vienna and one of Beethoven's first patrons.

♦ **LICHNOWSKY**
Already a patron of Mozart, he aligned himself to Beethoven as well. He hosted Beethoven in his home and, from 1800 to 1806, lavished upon him an annual contribution of 600 florins.

♦ **THE VIRTUOSO**
He who demonstrated extraordinary ability at the keyboard was often the principal attraction of the aristocracy's musical evenings.

♦ THE VIRTUOSOS
The relative novelty of an instrument such as the piano promoted the assertion for virtuosity, or rather a certain pomp towards oneself, from the part of the pianist for his actual ability on the keyboard. In Vienna the passion for the virtuoso encompassed all the social classes— one could find piano virtuosos at middle class festivals as well as in the most exclusive aristocratic halls. The success of performers such as Cramer, Wölfl, and Gelinek (pictured above, in an engraving from the epoch) was enormous: They were admired and protected, sought after as teachers, and often rivalries broke out between their patrons that were so heated that they led to the organization of true pianistic challenges. Beethoven was confronted with some of the best virtuosos of Vienna in some of these contests, which he conquered, above all, by his capacity to improvise.

♦ THE COUNTESS AND BEETHOVEN A rebel spirit, Beethoven presented himself in slovenly attire, refusing to play in spite of the urgings of Countess Thun.

4. THE LIFE OF BEETHOVEN ♦ *Strengthened by the presentation of Count Waldstein, his protector at Bonn, Beethoven succeeded in entering the best salons of Viennese high aristocracy, where he was appreciated above all as a piano virtuoso. In 1795 he submitted to the publisher Artaria his first composition with an opus number,* Trios for Piano, Violin, and Cello. *In the same year he made his debut before the Viennese people in a public concert for charity.* ⟫▸

THE CENTURY OF THE PIANO

◆ MUSIC STORES
The burgeoning of music stores, which offered instruments and musical scores, was due above all to the profusion of dilettantism within the bourgeoisie.

By the beginning of the 1800s, the piano had already replaced the older harpsichord and had earned the favor of the European nobility and bourgeoisie. In Vienna the public concerts featured, with ever-increasing frequency, sonatas or concertos for the piano, while virtuosic competitions in private salons were at their height. The number of dilettantes grew, as did the number of piano teachers. The publication of sonatas for the piano had by now greatly surpassed the publication of other more prestigious genres; finally, the habit, shunned by Beethoven, of rewriting for the piano compositions originally conceived for the orchestra, was consolidated.

◆ THE SALE OF PIANOS
The sale of a piano was often tied to the success of public concerts or of private musical evenings that featured the piano at the center.

◆ THE QUALITY OF THE PRESS
Because of the grave economic crisis resulting from the ravages of the Napoleonic Wars, the years between the 1700s and the 1800s saw a progressive regression in the quality of printing. From the smooth and white page with ample margins that was typical of the 1700s, the quality reverted at the beginning of the 1800s to a coarse paper and an ink that was between gray and pale green. The printing became more and more stock, and the frontispieces heavily decorated. Exceptions were a few Austrian, German, and English editions, embellished with elegant designs. Above and below, two scores from the era.

◆ STUDENTS
It is estimated that in Vienna piano students numbered about 6,000, mainly children of the high bourgeoisie.

◆ **THE MAESTROS**
In Vienna, there were about 300 teachers, attracted by the capital's enormous musical demand.

◆ **HISTORICAL EDITIONS**
In 1798, the publisher Breitkopf & Härtel began the publication of the complete works of Mozart and Haydn.

◆ **THE PUBLIC'S FAVORITES**
The works of Mozart and Haydn, and later Beethoven, most appealed to the tastes of the Viennese. There was renewed interest also in Händel, while at the end of the 1700s Bach did not yet enjoy great popularity.

EXHIBITIONS

The composer who aspired to make his music known to a broader public than the social and intellectual elite that frequented the salons of the aristocracy could organize an exhibition, that is, a concert open to a paying public. While in London there already existed a consolidated season of public concerts, in Vienna the exhibitions took place only during the Christmas season and Holy Week, when the theaters interrupted their operatic and prose activities. The program of public concerts was often varied and always very long: soloists, orchestra, and choir members alternated in virtual musical marathons of an average duration of three hours.

♦ **THE CONCLUSION OF THE EVENING**
In the exhibition of December 22, 1808, at the Theater an der Wien, Beethoven concluded the evening's program with the *Fantasia* for the piano, chorus, and orchestra.

♦ **THE EXHIBITION OF 1808**
In his career, Beethoven succeeded in organizing only eleven exhibitions for his own benefit. As far as the importance of the works presented, that of December 22, 1808, at the Theater an der Wien was memorable. On a freezing night, the few Viennese who hastened to the theater heard for the first time two symphonies, the *Fifth* and the *Sixth;* a concerto for the piano and orchestra, the *Fourth Concerto;* an aria and two movements from the *Mass in C;* a long piano improvisation by Beethoven; and finally, a *Fantasia* for the piano, chorus, and orchestra. The length of the program and the difficulty of the music strained not only the audience but the instrumentalists and chorus members as well. They repeatedly produced false notes in the *Fantasia,* provoking Beethoven's ire, and he forced them to repeat the piece from the beginning. Above, playbill of an exhibition.

♦ **THE MEMBERS OF THE CHORUS**
The insertion of a chorus in an instrumental piece, as provided in the *Fantasia Chorus,* was an innovation that Beethoven reintroduced in the *Ninth Symphony.*

♦ **ORCHESTRA**
The relationship between the orchestra and Beethoven was dismal. Dissatisfied with the performance of the instrumentalists, during rehearsals the composer often ended up insulting them.

The exhibitions
were announced
as being for charity
or were organized
by the composer
himself who,
after paying the
expenses, kept
the proceeds.

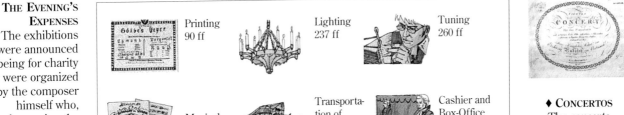

 Printing
90 ff

Lighting
237 ff

 Tuning
260 ff

 Musical
Scores
130 ff

Transporta-
tion of
Instruments
50 ff

Cashier and
Box-Office
Attendant
8 ff

♦ THE AUDIENCE
It was put to a very
hard test. A four-
hour concert, from

6:30 P.M. to
10:30 P.M., in
an unheated
theater.

♦ CONCERTOS
The *concerto*
is a composition
for a soloist and
orchestra (even
though this term
is often used to
indicate a general
musical perfor-
mance). It is the
genre with which
Beethoven
was frequently
associated.
His repertoire
consisted of seven
concertos—five
for the piano; one
for the violin; and
finally, one for
piano, violin, cello,
and orchestra.
Beethoven's
concerto work
knew first a
youthful phase,
more respectful
of tradition, and a
second more
mature one, more
innovative. To
this second phase
belong the
*Concertos for
Piano No. 4 and
No. 5,* in which
Beethoven intro-
duced an impor-
tant innovation
of form: the
orchestra did
not carry out the
sole function of
accompanying the
solo instrument,
but was involved
in a rich and
well-balanced
dialogue with
it. Above,
frontispiece of
*Concerto
No. 4 Op. 58.*

ROMANTICISM

Romanticism is a literary, artistic, and philosphical movement that was born in Germany at the end of the 1700s and then spread throughout much of Europe. Romanticism represented a moment of great renewal in European culture. Against the empty repetition of ancient models, typical of literary classicism, the Romantic movement exalted originality and individual expression; it preferred irrationality and contradictions to equilibrium and proportion of forms, and reason was replaced by sentiment, judged to be more useful in penetrating the most profound secrets of things.

♦ **THE JENA CIRCLE**
The birth of Romanticism can be traced to the experience and attention of a group of young German intellectuals that formed, between 1798 and 1800, a circle that has been passed down in history as the Coterie of Jena. Chief among the group were the brothers Friedrich and August Wilhelm Schlegel, along with their respective wives, Dorothea Mendelssohn and Karoline Michaelis, who were then joined by the poets Novalis and Tieck. The group founded a periodical, the *Athäneum,* which proclaimed the principal positions of the Romantic movement. To its usually new contents, the *Athäneum* added a certain agressiveness of expression, which gave rise to discussion and sometimes irritation among even giants of German literature such as Goethe and Schiller. Above, Caspar D. Freidrich, *Wanderer Above the Sea of Fog,* 1818, detail.

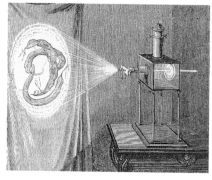

♦ **THE MAGIC LANTERN**
It appeared during the 1600s and 1700s and was perfected by Father Kircher (1645). It has been considered the ancestor of modern projection appliances. Above, an eighteenth-century engraving.

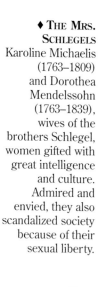

♦ **THE MRS. SCHLEGELS**
Karoline Michaelis (1763–1809) and Dorothea Mendelssohn (1763–1839), wives of the brothers Schlegel, women gifted with great intelligence and culture. Admired and envied, they also scandalized society because of their sexual liberty.

• **TIECK**
German poet and novelist, friend of Wackenroder and Novalis, German medieval poetry scholar, and, with August Schlegel, translator of the entire works of Shakespeare.

◆ **AN EVENING IN THE SCHLEGEL HOME**
In the home of the couple August Schlegel and Karoline Michaelis there took place an interesting and pleasant meeting of the Jena Circle. The wives of the brothers Schlegel staged a showing of Shakespeare's *The Tempest* with the magic lantern.

◆ **THE BROTHERS SCHLEGEL**
August Wilhelm (1767–1845) and Friedrich Schlegel (1772–1829) were the principal theorists of Romanticism. The former was a literary critic; the latter, a philologist and also a novelist.

◆ **NOVALIS**
(1772–1801) German poet of multiple personalities, he died at the young age of 29. Author of one of the most famous anthologies of German poetry, *Hymns to the Night,* inspired by a profound mystical mood.

◆ **ROMANTICISM AND MUSIC**
Literary and philosophical Romanticism can make the claim of having validated music and of having affirmed its primacy among the arts. Even in the full 1700s, instrumental music, unlike vocal music, was criticized for being obscure and incomprehensible. But for the Romantics, instrumental music had its own language, different from verbal language and even more efficacious. The reflections of the young Romantic critic Wackenroder and of the philosopher Schelling (above) were among the first important contributions to this idea. Both declared the superior capacity of music in expressing the most profound sentiments of man and in leading the individual toward the Absolute or to a more profound reality than the one faced in the here and now.

WAR AND PEACE

For almost twenty years (1796–1815), Europe was an enormous battlefield where Napoleon's French troops confronted the coalition composed of the armies of the ancient European monarchies. At stake in the conflict was the rule of the continent; the consequences were mainly devastation and economic crises. The absolute protagonist of these years was Napoleon Bonaparte; a French general who distinguished himself in the Italian campaign (1796–1797), after a series of almost uninterrupted military victories, won in the name of the principles of the Revolution. He betrayed the republican ideals, proclaiming himself Emperor of the French and exercising absolute power over much of Europe.

♦ **MUZIO CLEMENTI**
In a Europe upset by war, one musician enjoyed the privilege of being able to cross opposing fronts by virtue of a pass awarded him by Napoleon as well as his enemies. This musician was the Italian Muzio Clementi (1752–1832), above. Piano virtuoso, rival of Mozart in a memorable competition before Emperor Joseph II, he supported his activity as a soloist by composing. Moving to London at a very young age, Clementi grounded himself in the composition of symphonies and, above all, piano sonatas. Following a successful tour of the major European capitals (1802–1810), Clementi returned to London where he dedicated himself to the activities of publisher and piano builder.

♦ **THE BATTLE OF AUSTERLITZ**
December 2, 1805: the Battle of Austerlitz, also called the Battle of Three Emperors. Between Brünn and Austerlitz the French army, commanded by Napoleon, confronted the Austro-Russian troops. On this occasion, Napoleon revealed his great strategic qualities as well as his capacity to galvanize the morale of his troops.

♦ **NAPOLEON**
He was born in Ajaccio, Corsica, in 1769 and died in exile on the island of Saint Helena in 1821.

♦ **THE ARMIES** Confronting the well-prepared Napoleonic troops were the armies of the different coalitions established between 1796 and 1815 to oppose France. They consisted of the great powers of Europe: Austria, England, Russia, and Prussia. From the left, the uniform of the respective armies.

♦ **BERNADOTTE** French marshal, in 1798 ambassador to Vienna. Here he suggested to Beethoven the idea of a symphony on Bonaparte.

♦ **THE ARTILLERY** Technologically advanced, the French artillery primarily boasted a better organization: it differentiated between battle cannons, which were lighter, and those used for siege or fortress, which were of greater caliber.

♦ **THE DEDICATION OF THE THIRD SYMPHONY** Beethoven, like the philosopher Kant and the writers Goethe and Schiller, developed a great admiration for Napoleon as a result of both his engaging personality and because he seemed to represent the armed branch of republican ideas against the monarchical tradition. In 1803 Beethoven decided to dedicate *Symphony No. 3* to the Corsican general. But the offer by Prince Lobkowitz of 400 florins in exchange for a dedication caused him to change his mind about dedicating it to Napoleon; however, he did entitle it *Bonaparte*. However, in 1804, when the republican Beethoven learned that Napoleon had proclaimed himself Emperor, he ripped the frontispiece of the symphony, renouncing the title *Bonaparte* in favor of the definitive title *Eroica* (above, the frontispiece).

5. THE LIFE OF BEETHOVEN ♦ *By the century's end, Beethoven was considered one of the most fascinating composers on the Viennese musical scene. Five different publishers competed for his works, while the Viennese aristocracy venerated and coddled him. In 1800 he organized his first public concert with proceeds going to him. From this year on, Prince Lichnowsky awarded Beethoven an annual salary of 600 florins, thus freeing him from any economic worry.* ⧉›

THE COMPOSER'S LABORATORY

Beethoven was the first musician to consider his own music as an elevated art that required an extraordinary commitment both on the part of the composer as well as the listener: neither Mozart nor Haydn dared to suggest this. He therefore dedicated a great deal of time to composing: to the initial ideas that may have come to him in any locality, and that he wrote down immediately in his notebook, he added a lengthy labor of selection and correction in the privacy of his own study.

♦ **THE PIANO SONATAS**
The popularity of Ludwig van Beethoven is tied to a few piano sonatas that for various reasons have distinguished themselves among his contemporaries. Among these we note *Op. 13,* entitled *Pathétique,* on account of the intimate and sentimental mood of the adagio; *Op. 27, Moonlight Sonata,* for the dreamy character also of the adagio; *Op. 53,* called *Waldstein;* and *Op. 57, Appassionata,* for the vigorous sound and the stylistic innovations introduced by the composer. Perturbation and skepticism were the forces behind *Sonata Op. 106,* called *Hammerklavier.* Imposing and full of difficulties, it would be fully appreciated only by future generations of musicians and fans. Above, gold binding of the *Piano Sonata in D Major Op. 28.*

♦ **THE TIME OF CREATIVITY**
Beethoven spent many hours in his study working: from dawn to noon and, after an afternoon rest, from early evening until late at night.

♦ **THE SONATAS**
Beethoven's favorite area of experimentation with forms that were welcomed even in the genres of the symphony and the string quartet.

♦ **THE BUYERS**
Beethoven also composed music for special occasions and entertainment pieces for various purchasers. This work occupied Beethoven for a very brief time.

♦ **THE NOTEBOOKS**
Beethoven recorded his musical ideas in notebooks. We have about fifty of them (at left, one from 1818), which testify to his long and thoughtful creative processes.

♦ **THE QUARTETS**
Beethoven paid particular attention to the quartets, a prestigious and cultured musical genre and therefore assigned to the most engaging music.

♦ **THE LIBRARY**
Beethoven's musical library consisted of Clementi's entire musical works for the piano, half of the score of Mozart's *Don Giovanni,* Bach's *Well-Tempered Clavier,* and some of Palestrina's Masses.

♦ **THE SYMPHONIES**
Mozart composed 52 symphonies; Haydn, 108; and Beethoven, only nine. Such a difference in number is explained by the unprecedented need of the composer to rework again and again until the result was satisfactory.

Music and Nature

Beethoven found in nature an extraordinary stimulus to his creativity. The meadows and country air stimulated his imagination. It was not unlikely to find him climbing the branches of a tree searching for inspiration. But for Beethoven, nature also had a profoundly religious significance: it was the reflection of God. His love for nature and the sacred in nature were effectively combined in Beethoven's *Sixth Symphony,* entitled *Pastoral.* Composed in Vienna between 1807 and 1808, it was inspired by Beethoven's long sojourns in Heiligenstadt, a suburb north of Vienna, surrounded by dense forests.

♦ **The Tempest**
4. In the fourth movement, the roll of the timpani and the blare of brass instruments represented lightning and thunder. The symphony lived through one of its most tense moments.

♦ **The Peasants**
3. The third movement, "The Gathering of Country Folk," a vivacious scherzo in a dance tempo illustrated a happy country festival.

♦ **The Stream**
2. The second movement was entitled "The Stream." North of Heiligenstadt there is a stream, from whose northern shore departs "Beethoven's Path," in remembrance of the composer's many walks there.

6. The Life of Beethoven ♦ *There appeared in 1798 the first symptoms of deafness. They became progressively more pronounced and dragged Beethoven to the crisis of 1802 at Heiligenstadt, a suburb of Vienna, where, prey to the blackest depression, he virtually contemplated suicide. Having overcome the difficult moment, Beethoven immersed himself in his work, inaugurating a new phase of his creative period. In 1803, he composed the* Third Symphony, *a revolutionary work that condensed the new Beethoven style, called "heroic."* ➠➤

THE PASTORAL
It is composed of five corresponding movements to five different moments of country life.

• THE SHEPHERD'S SONG
5. With the fifth movement, the tension that had built up during the storm is dissipated. Beethoven concluded with a song of thanks to God.

♦ THE HEILIGENSTADT TESTAMENT
After Beethoven's death, among the papers found in his home was a letter that became famous as the *Heiligenstadt Testament* (above, a handwritten page). Written by hand by Beethoven himself, it carried the date 1802 and was addressed to his two brothers. Beethoven confessed to them the drama of his own deafness. The first symptoms of his illness had manifested themselves in 1798, but in 1802 the problem became more serious. With sincere anguish Beethoven explained how the illness separated him from men and risked compromising his work as a musician. Beethoven declared, however, that he wished to fight his despair with his art, which was a vocation, the work of a lifetime. The years following the writing of the *Heiligenstadt Testament* were, in fact, musically prolific for Beethoven.

♦ "AWAKENING OF IMPRESSIONS"
1. This is the title of the first movement. The *Pastoral* is not only the description of various events but also the expression of the personal sentiments of the composer regarding nature.

♦ INSTRUMENT–ANIMAL CORRESPONDENCE
In the *Pastoral*, Beethoven reproduced the song of the nightingale, the quail, and the cuckoo, relying on the flute, the oboe, and the clarinet, respectively.

UNDER THE LAW

In 1803 the publisher Artaria brought Beethoven to court in a case of defamation regarding a quintet that the musician had sold first to him and then to Breitkopf & Härtel of Leipzig. Judicial cases between publishers and composers were rare, especially since no law existed regarding either the rights of authorship, to which the musician could have appealed, or a norm against an unauthorized publication, which defended the publisher against pirated copies. It therefore occurred that a composer could sell the score to one publisher and then, once the work was published, to other publishers, usually in foreign countries. Others then copied the score without paying either the composer or the original publisher possessing the print rights.

♦ **THE EPISODE OF NEPHEW KARL**
On November 15, 1815, Caspar Carl, brother of Ludwig, died. He had expressed the wish that the guardianship of his son Karl (above) be shared by both his wife and Beethoven. But the composer asked the court to grant him sole guardianship of his nephew. Supported by his influencial acquaintances within the aristocracy, he quickly obtained it, beginning a lengthy legal dispute with his sister-in-law Johanna. After passing from the court of nobles to the civil magistrate, and various other episodes, Beethoven obtained definitive guardianship in 1820. But the favorable verdict did not ensure him a serene family life; rather, it was the beginning of a difficult relationship with his nephew: Karl often ran away from home and in 1826 even attempted to take his own life.

♦ **BEETHOVEN VERSUS MÄLZEL**
In 1815 Beethoven and Mälzel ended up in court over the ownership of the *Wellington's Sieg* (above, frontispiece of the original edition), a work originally written by Beethoven for an orchestra of automatons constructed by Mälzel.

♦ **ARTARIA VERSUS BEETHOVEN**
The municipal court dealt with the Artaria–Beethoven case. Artaria presented before the tribunal a petition demanding public apologies of Beethoven, who had accused him of stealing *Quintet Op. 29*.

♦ **ARTARIA**
Among the major European publishers, Domenico Artaria brought legal action against Beethoven to defend the good name of his publishing house and to discourage any more tricks on the part of other musicians.

7. THE LIFE OF BEETHOVEN ♦ *In 1803, the Theater an der Wein commissioned Beethoven to compose an opera, and, in addition, allowed the composer to announce in that same year an exhibition to benefit himself. The Beethoven Exhibition, which took place on April 5, 1803, became part of the ferocious, unrestrained fight between Schikaneder, director of the An der Wein, and Baron von Braun, director of the imperial theaters. On the very night of Beethoven's exhibition, in fact, von Braun had scheduled at the Kärnterthor a revival of Haydn's oratorio* The Creation, *assuring him the city's best musicians.* ⫸⭢

♦ **BEETHOVEN**
In spite of the fact that Beethoven was forced to admit that he had personally corrected the galleys of the very quintet in Artaria's lawful possession, he would never retract his accusations.

♦ **MUSICAL PIRACY**
An imperial decree of 1775 prohibited the unauthorized copying of works printed in Austria. However, no such protection existed for musical scores printed outside of the empire.

♦ **THE TRIBUNALS**
In the Austrian State, still organized according to the ancient order, there existed different laws and courts for the nobility and bourgeoisie. The former were judged by the Landrecht, while the latter were judged by the Magistracy.

♦ **ATTORNEY BACH**
Defending Beethoven was probably the same legal clerk who would also assist him in the case of his nephew's guardianship.

FIDELIO

Although instrumental music was by now undermining the primacy of vocal music, the opera was still the genre of greatest prestige. Between 1804 and 1805, Beethoven wrote *Fidelio;* it is a singspiel, which is a theatrical opera written in the German language consisting of sung parts and recited parts. Set in the 1600s in the state prison of Seville, it tells of the courage and virtue of Leonore, the wife of Florestan, who is illegally imprisoned by Governor Pizarro. After having dressed up as a man and bearing the name Fidelio, Leonore goes to the prison to gather information about her husband. Finding him in chains and weakened with hunger, she rescues him from Pizarro, who wishes to kill him for fear that the minister who is arriving will uncover his machinations.

♦ **THE GENESIS OF FIDELIO**
There exist three versions of the opera. This first, of 1805, with a libretto by Sonnleithner (above), is in four acts. Performed at the Theater an der Wien, during the full French occupation, it was removed from the program after two performances. Together with his friend Stephan von Breuning, Beethoven wrote a second version, performed in 1806, with a new overture and the fusion of the first two acts into a single one. Its reception was still lukewarm. In 1814, Beethoven's renewed popularity convinced the director of the Kärntnerthor Theater to revive *Fidelio.* For the occasion, Beethoven, with the new librettist Treitschke, modified the opera, including more action and inserting a new finale, containing the famous "Prisoners' Hymn."

♦ **THE MINISTER FERNANDO**
Also about to arrive in the story is the Minister Fernando, who will arrest Pizarro, praising Leonore for her courage.

♦ **LEONORE**
Devoted wife of Florestan, under the assumed name of Fidelio, she wins the trust of Rocco, the warden, who hires her as an assistant.

♦ **FLORESTAN**
Husband of Leonore and political adversary of Pizarro, he finds himself in prison for having denounced the intrigues.

♦ **CHERUBINI**
At the première of *Fidelio,* Luigi Cherubini, the French composer of Italian origin and a leading exponent of French Revolution opera was present. Beethoven looked to his operas as models.

♦ **PIZARRO**
Upon learning of the arrival of the minister Don Fernando, the cruel governor goes to Florestan's cell with the intention of killing him, but Leonore intervenes, placing herself between him and her husband.

♦ **THE FINALE**
This is the opera's most dramatic moment. Pizarro wishes to kill Florestan, but Leonore rescues her own husband, threatening the governor of the prison with a pistol. The trumpets blare announcing the arrival of the minister.

♦ **ROCCO AND MARCELLINA**
Rocco is the warden of the prison. A simple and obedient man, he encourages his daughter Marcellina, who wishes to marry Fidelio, that is, Leonore in disguise.

♦ **REVOLUTION OPERAS**
An important work of the new revolutionary *opèra-comique, Fidelio* was born of a French libretto, Bouilly's *Léonore,* and set to music by Gaveaux. Beethoven was a fan of neither the Italian *opera buffa,* on account of its frivolity and the "immorality" of its librettos, nor of *opera seria,* which he deemed too full of ancient heroes and mythological characters. Contrarily, he was enthusiastic about the new French opera, where the realism of the setting blended with the serious-ness of the subject. *Fidelio* belongs, moreover, to a typical genre of French Revolution operas, that of the *opèra au savetage,* a drama where the good and noble character, threatened by the external wicked man, saves himself through an act of exceptional courage rather than as the result of a divine providential intervention. Above, Cherubini's *Medea* at Milan's La Scala.

♦ **FRENCH OFFICIALS**
The première of *Fidelio* took place a week after the Occupation of Vienna by Napoleon's troops (November 20, 1805). Several French officials were in the half-empty stalls.

THE IMMORTAL BELOVED

Love is a painful and mysterious chapter in the life of Beethoven. He often fell in love with his young and aristocratic students who appreciated his friendship and company, but who had difficulty becoming his lovers. He threw himself into impossible amorous situations that on the one hand caused him to pine away, but on the other hand freed him for what Beethoven considered his only true mission, music. Beethoven's emotional life was tinged with a bit of yellow (as in yellow journalism) upon the discovery of one of the composer's letters addressed to a mysterious immortal lover, that gave rise to the most diverse hypotheses as to her identity.

♦ **JOSEPH II**

♦ **NAPOLEON**

♦ **THE IMMORTAL BELOVED**
Among the papers found in Beethoven's house after his death was a letter addressed to a mysterious immortal beloved. Her identity is a subject that impassions scholars to this day. At the end of the 1800s, the theory prevailed that the recipient of the letter was Countess Therese von Brunswick, while in more recent years an English scholar seems to have demonstrated that the immortal beloved was actually Antonia Brentano (above, in a portrait). The search is also particularly difficult because the date of the letter is uncertain. It was composed in three parts, written on three different days: Beethoven recounted to her the inconveniences of a trip, but above all abandoned himself to direct declarations of love and floods of passion.

♦ **THE HUSBAND**
A Hungarian count, exiled for having killed someone in a duel, he arrived in Vienna under the pseudonym of Müller.

♦ **JOSEPHINE**
In 1799, she was Beethoven's student, and she fell in love with him. But because of the poor economic conditions of her family she was convinced by her mother to marry Count Deym.

♦ **MECHANICAL DEVICES**
The Viennese adored mechanisms that emitted music. A carillon could be found in every home of the capital.

♦ **THE MANUSCRIPT**
Lied with six *Variations WoO 74 "Approach of the Lover"* for piano (four hands), dedicated to Josephine (Deym) and Therese von Brunswick.

♦ **THE PALACE OF THE COUNT**
Someone advanced the theory that the immortal beloved could be Josephine Brunswick, married to Count Deym in 1799. He possessed an enormous palace with eighty rooms, in which he had prepared a museum of wax statues and mechanical musical devices.

♦ **MOZART**

♦ **THE WAX STATUES**
These were a favorite diversion of the Viennese. The gallery of Count Deym was, along with that of Dubsky at the Prater, the most important in Vienna.

♦ **BEETHOVEN AND HIS BELOVED**
Beethoven continued to give Josephine piano lessons, even after her marriage to Count Deym.

8. THE LIFE OF BEETHOVEN ♦ *In 1805, the amorous relationship of Beethoven with Josephine Brunswick, widow of Count Deym for a year, was by now public domain. The two spent many hours of the day together. After a while, however, their relationship began to erode until its rupture in 1807. Between 1806 and 1808, Beethoven's repertoire was expanded with several masterpieces of what belong to the so-called heroic style:* the Fifth Symphony *and the group of* Quartets *called* Rasoumovsky Op. 59. ⇒

THE SYMPHONIES

Beethoven tackled the symphonic genre at about the age of thirty, an advanced age compared to the masters of Viennese classicism, Haydn and Mozart. His rigid self-discipline and his almost religious respect for the genre of the symphony had convinced him that only upon achieving a solid stylistic maturity could he undertake such a difficult enterprise. After his first two attempts, traditional and transitional, with the *Third Symphony,* entitled *Eroica,* Beethoven shook up the established forms of Viennese classicism and gave birth to a new style in terms of the structure of the musical bar, composition forms, and the search for sounds.

♦ **THE NINE SYMPHONIES**
Symphony No. 1 in C Major and *No. 2 in D Major* remain tied to the model of the Viennese masters. *No. 3 in E Flat Major* represents, on the other hand, a courageous break with both the past and present symphonic genre. *No. 4 in B Flat Major* is a return to the forms already discussed in *Eroica. No. 5 in C Minor* is among Beethoven's most representative symphonies, both for its rhythmic energy and its thematic elaboration. *No. 6 in F Major* invalidates the thematic contrasts present in the *Third Symphony,* and the *Fourth Symphony. No. 7 in A Major* is the exaltation of dance. *Symphony No. 8 in F Major* is shorter. And finally, *No. 9, in D Minor* is the masterpiece of his maturity. Above, Herbert von Karajan, orchestra conductor, sublime interpreter of Beethoven's symphonies.

♦ **BEETHOVEN'S ORCHESTRA**
Beethoven did not enlarge the staff of the orchestra used by Haydn and Mozart, but he profoundly modified his use of it.

♦ **THE HORNS**
Even though he did not enlarge the orchestral staff, now and again Beethoven added a few instruments to function as soloists. This was the case with the third horn in *Eroica,* employed with great care and parsimony.

♦ **THE VIOLINS**
They lost their ancient role as exhibitors of the principal theme. In *Symphony No. 2,* for example, Beethoven entrusted the principal theme to the cellos and contrabasses and only secondarily to the violins.

♦ **THE WOODWINDS**
Beethoven entrusted the presentation of the theme to various instruments; the timbre of the symphony was thus enriched. The woodwinds, in particular, lost their ancient function of harmonic support to participate in the thematic elaboration.

♦ **THE TIMPANI**
Besides their normal function of providing rhythmic background, they could participate in the presentation of a brief motif. The brevity of rhythmic themes often characterized Beethoven's symphonies.

♦ **THE STYLE**
Beethoven introduced a symphonic style that was respectful of tradition and at the same time innovative. He adopted the composition model of Viennese classicism: four movements, the first and last in the sonata or rondo form, but he inserted so many rhythmic and harmonic exceptions that it became difficult to say whether or not one was still dealing with the classical style. One important innovation of Beethoven's symphonies was their amplitude: *Eroica,* for example, lasts fifty minutes, twice the length of a Haydn symphony. What was expanded was mainly the development section in which Beethoven's themes, often brief and rhythmic, were enriched with surprising solutions that maintained the tension until the dénouement of the recapitulation. Above, Beethoven conducting.

♦ **THE CONDUCTOR**
The growing complexity of symphonic works gave rise to the birth of the orchestra conductor. Previously the scansion of time was a task carried out by the first violin.

♦ **VIOLAS AND CELLOS**
In Beethoven's symphonies, the development acquired greater weight, with violas and cellos playing an important role.

POPULAR MUSIC

In the German squares and inns, popular music has never disappeared, but rather has been handed down and revised through the centuries. In the first years of the 1800s, however, there occurred a new phenomenon: an interest in history, culture, and popular art on the part of cultured artists and intellectuals. It was mainly the Romantic writers who discovered and collected a vast repertoire of stories and popular songs, convinced that the original character of the German nation, and therefore of its people, would be found precisely in that ancient legacy.

♦ THE BOY'S MAGIC HORN
Between 1806 and 1808, Achim von Arnim (1781–1831) and Clemens Brentano (1778–1842)—above, in a portrait—two young German poets, collected more than 700 ancient popular German songs and published them in a volume entitled *The Boy's Magic Horn.* The collection consisted of songs of various origins and periods. The majority had anonymous authorship and they were at times subjected to the arbitrary revisions of von Arnim and Brentano. These two intended to demonstrate that the genuine simplicity of the German people and the superiority of their values were expressed in the rich tradition of popular song. The collection therefore entered into the climate, inaugurated by Romanticism, of the discovery and validation of the nation's past.

♦ THE MASTER SINGER
Through the centuries, he was the zealous trustee of popular German music, immortalized by the writer Goethe and the composer Wagner. Above, the great chorus scene of Wagner's opera *The Master Singers.*

♦ TIGHTROPE WALKERS
Acrobats were one of the principal attractions at country festivals.

♦ CULTURED MUSICIANS
In their search for ideas and inspirations, they often mingled willingly with the crowd.

♦ THE POLICE
They made sure that the enthusiasm of the festival participants did not turn into disorder and anarchy.

♦ THE FESTIVAL
In a suburb of Vienna a popular festival took place, where the spontaneous enthusiasm of peasants and artisans blended with the consummate ability of street artists.

♦ BEETHOVEN AND POPULAR MUSIC
Even Beethoven enhanced European popular music. In 1807, the Scottish publisher George Thompson (above) commissioned him to arrange popular Irish and Welsh songs, later published in 1814. Two years later, Beethoven composed new harmonizations of popular European songs for Thompson's publishing house, among them a Swedish lullaby, Tyrolese arias, and a Venetian song.

♦ POPULAR DANCE
In addition to the *ländler,* a typical popular Austrian dance, the mazurka was danced, which originated in Poland and spread throughout the popular classes of all of Europe.

MEETING GOETHE

Divided politically, the German nation found itself united in its admiration for Goethe, poet, novelist, playwright, and universal philosopher. Beethoven, who was himself the glory of German art and in his youth an impassioned reader of Goethe, wished to meet the great intellectual. The meeting took place in 1812 at Teplitz, a Bohemian thermal spa, and seemed to open important prospects for German vocal music: in fact, Beethoven suggested to Goethe that he set his *Faust* to music. But the two men disliked each other, thus setting to rest the possibility of their collaboration.

◆ **GOETHE**
He was born in Frankfurt in 1749 to a rich family. A law student, he cultivated more diverse interests, from painting to medicine, concentrating primarily on literature. Not yet twenty-four years old and already the author of poetry collections and a few plays, Goethe wrote *The Sorrows of Young Werther,* an epistolary novel that would have extraordinary success and that would become the symbol of the new European youth. Other masterpieces followed, such as the novel, *Meister Wilhelm* and the play *Egmont.* Moving to Weimar, he was appointed director of the court theater and became a close friend of Schiller. He died in 1832, after having completed *Faust,* his life's work, begun in 1773. Above, an engraving of Goethe on a 1778 edition of *The Sorrows of Young Werther.*

◆ **TEPLITZ**
A Bohemian thermal spa, it was frequented by the aristocracy of the Empire. On July 21, 1812, Goethe and Beethoven ran into each other at the imperial procession.

◆ **ARCHDUKE RUDOLPH**
Cadet brother of the Emperor of Austria, at the age of sixteen, he was Beethoven's student. In 1809, he was one of the underwriters of the contract that guaranteed Beethoven a generous annuity.

◆ **ZELTER**
Composer, Goethe's friend and trusted musical advisor. He composed *lieder* based on Goethe's verses.

● **THE THERMAL BATHS**
At Teplitz, there were radioactive thermal springs due to volcanic phenomena present in the region.

◆ **THE CURE FOR DEAFNESS**
Beethoven entrusted himself to charlatans who promised definitive cures. Distinguishing himself for his strictness and caution, however, was Doctor Schmidt, a personal friend of the composer. Above, a nineteenth-century print.

◆ **GOETHE**
As soon as the great Goethe saw the imperial procession, he removed his hat and bowed.

◆ **BEETHOVEN**
Remaining haughtily seated, Beethoven mocked Goethe's behavior.

9. THE LIFE OF BEETHOVEN ◆ *Beethoven's economic position improved in 1809 when Archduke Rudolph and the Princes Lobkowitz and Kinsky drew up a contract that bound the three aristocrats to turn over a generous financial sum to Beethoven annually in order to allow him to freely create his art. This economic independence was of short duration, however: the recent French Occupation of Vienna (1809) provoked a severe devaluation of Austrian money, which cut in half the value of the money assured him by his patrons.* ⟫→

STAGE MUSIC

On the strength of its innovation, Romanticism even influenced prose theater. A greater liberty, in content but above all in form, replaced the rigid rules that classicism had imposed, in particular the compulsory unity of time and place. Among the most important innovations was the growing presence of stage music. Beethoven competed even in this musical genre. He composed stage music for Joseph von Collin's *Coriolan* (1807) and for Goethe's *Egmont* (1809).

♦ **BEETHOVEN'S STAGE MUSIC**
Stage music is articulated in various forms: the overture, a musical piece that precedes the curtain raising; instrumental intermissions that separate the various acts or scenery changes; and the melo-logue, the intervention of the orchestra as a background to the characters' monologues or dialogues. The music composed by Beethoven for *Egmont* (1809) was the richest and most well-thought-out of his repertoire. It included an overture, four intermissions, two arias, and a symphony. For *Coriolan* (1807) Beethoven composed an overture, while for *Leonore Prohaska* (1815) he wrote a chorus, a ballad, a melologue, and even a funeral march. Above, an engraving of the period illustrating a scene in *Egmont*.

♦ **AGAINST THE RULES**
The Romantic theater renounced the obligation of setting a drama in only one place, as dictated by Aristotelian rules, a longtime model for European theater.

♦ **THE CANNONS**
The roar of the cannon in the theater was so popular that, to attract the public to the theater, impresarios announced in the inns the number of cannon fires included in a performance.

♦ **BEETHOVEN'S MUSIC IN FILM**
We recall the *Ninth Symphony* in *A Clockwork Orange* by the English director Kubrick (at right, a scene), and the symphony *Pastoral* in Walt Disney's animated film *Fantasia*.

♦ **ANIMALS**
The desire for the exotic led to the presence of camels in the theater, while battle scenes required the use of horses.

♦ **THREE-DIMENSIONAL OBJECTS**
Throughout the 1700s, back-drop drawings represented the setting; now, however, the stage was filled with actual objects while the back-drop provided only a background.

♦ **THE COSTUMES**
The necessity, dictated by the Romantic theater, of greater realism imposed an unprecedented attention to costumes.

THE AGE OF RESTORATION

With the definitive defeat of Napoleon at Waterloo (1815), the era of constant warfare was over, and the great powers prepared to restore the ancient order. In Vienna, kings, ministers, chancellors, and ambassadors came together to decide upon Europe's political destiny. But the Congress of Vienna was not only a political meeting of the highest level; it was also an occasion for an endless series of spectacles, displays, and above all dances. The new and extravagant Viennese ballrooms, a symbol of a renewed need for escape, hosted, often in disguise, crowned heads and diplomats.

♦ **HOT-AIR BALLOONS**
Among the more bizarre displays organized during the Congress was a hot-air balloon contest. Above, an engraving of the period.

♦ **THE SECRET POLICE**
In the relaxed atmosphere, they could gather information by listening to the chatter of the ambassadors.

♦ **THE WOMEN**
The secret police hired attractive young girls for the purpose of seducing the diplomats in order to extort useful secrets.

♦ **TALLEYRAND**
French Minister of Foreign Affairs, he had the difficult task at the Congress of defending the territorial integrity of France after its defeat.

♦ **THE CZAR**
By virtue of his fine appearance and majesty, Czar Alexander I was the most popular sovereign among the Viennese.

♦ THE CONGRESS
OF VIENNA

**♦ THE CONGRESS
OF VIENNA**
At the Congress
(above, a popular
print of the
epoch), held from
November 1814
to June 9, 1815,
216 delegations
were present,
representing
states and other
recognized
groups.
Regulating all of
them, however,
were the four
European powers:
Great Britain,
Russia, Prussia,
and Austria. They
would establish
Europe's new
political order,
inspired by two
fundamental
principles: a
return to their
thrones as legiti-
mate sovereigns
after the upsets
provoked by the
French Revolution
and by Napoleon,
and the establish-
ment of a firm
balance among
the powers.
The Austrian
Chancellor
Metternich and
Czar Alexander I
were further
concerned that
the return of the
ancient dynasties
be accompanied
by a strong social
restoration that
would do away
with the gains
achieved by the
bourgeoisie, and
once again
restored the
ancient privileges
of the nobility.

♦ CASTLEREAGH
English Minister
of Foreign
Affairs, cold
and impenetrable,
he provoked the
laughter of the
Viennese for
the secret waltz
lessons he took
with his wife.

♦ METTERNICH
The Austrian
Chancellor
organized
diversions for
his foreign guests
so as to exercise
greater control
over them.

10. THE LIFE OF BEETHOVEN ♦ *The years between 1813
and 1815 are glorious ones in Beethoven's professional
biography. To encourage the renewed nationalism of the
Viennese, Beethoven composed* Wellington's Sieg, *an
opera that celebrated the victory of the Duke of Wellington
in Spain against the French troops. Appealing to military
tastes, so widespread during this period, the work assured
the composer an extraordinary success. In November of
1814 the Congress of Vienna began, and Beethoven had
the opportunity, thanks to his influential acquaintances,
to meet the most important sovereigns of Europe, who
paid him homage.* ≫→

THE WALTZ

It was not by chance that during the years of the Restoration a dance as revolutionary as the waltz affirmed itself. Primarily an expression of the rising bourgeoisie (middle class), the waltz symbolized the unfeasibility of Metternich's restoration plan. In Vienna, in the public dance halls, but even in the salons of the aristocracy, this simple, liberal, and scandalous dance overshadowed popular dances and court dances. With their whirling spins, the young Viennese expressed their desire for escape but also their strong sense of freedom.

♦ ORIGIN AND DIFFUSION

The origin of the waltz is a popular dance, the *ländler,* born and spread in southern Germany: a dance in three-quarter time and of slow movement. By the end of the 1700s, the waltz dominated the German scene, differing from the *ländler* in its abandonment of the jumps and pirouettes and in its transferral from peasant festivals to ballroom salons. In Berlin, couples in each other's arms whirled around each other forming a circle every two bars, while in Vienna, a much more rapid waltz raged. The Viennese waltz would become the classic waltz, so fast and over-whelming that it produced intoxication and dizziness. The waltz involved all social classes, and its popularity was such that in Germany a study was published that sought to demonstrate the waltz's danger to the development of German youth. Above, detail of a nineteenth-century painting.

11. THE LIFE OF BEETHOVEN ♦ *Between 1814 and 1815, he won his case against the heirs Kinsky and Lobkowitz, who no longer intended to respect the contract of 1809. In 1815, Beethoven's brother Caspar Carl died, and Beethoven asked the court to grant him exclusive guardianship of his nephew. It is the beginning of a long legal dispute that would pit him against his sister-in-law. A year earlier, he had met the young Schindler who, from 1816 on became his secretary. His deafness meanwhile progressed: Beethoven resorted to ear trumpets, and a short while later conversation notebooks appeared, by which his guests communicated with him in writing.* ➡

♦ THE APOLLO BALLROOM
The Apollo was different from other Viennese ballrooms because of its smooth and polished floor that facilitated very rapid dancing.

♦ THE WALTZ IN MUSIC
The fathers of the Viennese waltz are Joseph Lanner and Johann Strauss Senior (1804–1849), the latter composer of the famous *Radetzky March*. To them is due the transformation of the original *ländler* into the classic Viennese waltz, brisk and lively, with an introduction in duple meter, followed by six parts in a waltz tempo, that is, a ternary and a coda that subjects the principal themes to an accelerated rhythm. In juxtaposition to the unrestrained velocity of the rhythm is an extremely simple melody. The legacy of the father is conserved and renewed by Johann Strauss, son (1825–1899)—above, in a portrait—author of the famous *Blue Danube.* He has the distinction of having given the waltz the dignity of a genre for a large orchestra, thereby including it in the prestigious tradition of Viennese symphony.

♦ THE EMBRACE
The waltz was viewed as suspect by the court that judged a dance scandalous that fostered physical contact by its dancers.

THE STRING QUARTETS

♦ **BEETHOVEN'S QUARTETS**
Beginning with his first youthful attempts, Beethoven's work in the genre of the quartet began in Vienna in 1795 with the commission to write a group of quartets. Published under opus number 18, they are still reminiscent of the legacy of Haydn and Mozart. More original, by contrast, are the three *Quartets Op. 59* dedicated to Rasoumovsky (above, in a portrait), composed between 1805 and 1806. Closer to Beethoven's new symphonic style, they surprised by the ampleness of their forms—no one had ever heard quartets of such long duration—and by a development section that was rich and extensive. After the *Quartet in E Flat Major* (1809) and the *Quartet in F Minor* (1810), Beethoven would wait almost fifteen years before tackling the genre once again. The results were so innovative that his contemporaries had difficulty comprehending their worth.

With Haydn and Mozart, the string quartet was revised and at the same time elevated: the rigid hierarchy that had dominated the genre until the end of the 1700s, based upon the first violin boasting primacy over the remaining instruments, disappeared. First violin, second violin, viola, and cello now had equal dignity: "The quartet is a conversation among four individuals of good sense," as Goethe used to say. Beethoven took this principle to heart and put it to the service of ever more original musical forms and ideas that in his last quartets (1824–1826) would appear virtually incomprehensible and scandalous.

♦ **THE FOURFOLD MUSIC STAND**
A bizarre and rather awkward Biedermeier object.

♦ **THE ENVIRONMENT**
The reestablished Schuppanzigh quartet performed one of Beethoven's works in the house of a rich Viennese financier.

♦ THE
SHUPPANZIG
QUARTET
The first profes-
sional quartet in
Vienna, founded
by Ignaz
Schuppanzig,
violinist and
friend of
Beethoven.
Disbanded in
1816, it resumed
activity seven
years later.

♦ QUARTETS
Beethoven
increased the
resonant power of
the quartet that
entered the con-
cert halls, without
its having to aban-
don more intimate
settings. Indeed,
the quartet
became the
favorite genre of
the ascending
bourgeoisie as
far as music to be
performed within
the family.

♦ BIEDERMEIER
This term defined
an epoch in which
a sober lifestyle
imposed itself
even among the
well-to-do classes.
It primarily influ-
enced a style of
furnishing that
became simple
and functional:
the round table
was favored
because it
accommodated
more people
seated around it.

THE ROSSINI CASE

While Beethoven was exploring new musical territories, separating himself from the common preferences and above all renouncing popularity, in Europe Gioacchino Rossini was making a name for himself as a composer of Italian opera. Without revising anything but rather relying on his own immense talent, Rossini garnered an astounding series of successes. When in 1822 Rossini, with an Italian company, settled in Vienna for a few performances of his operas, the Austrian capital went wild. The spectacles overflowed. The nobles practically came to blows with each other in order to host him in their palaces, while the more humble Viennese warmly applauded him when he walked through the streets.

♦ ROSSINI
(1792–1868)
Italian composer, he would long be the most famous and richest composer-musician in Europe. The operatic career of Rossini—above, in a portrait—began in Venice in 1810. After his initial successes, Barbaja, director of the San Carlo Theater in Naples, contracted him for several seasons as a permanent (house) composer. Rossini's Neopolitan operas (we recall *Otello, Moses in Egypt,* and *The Lady of the Lake*) achieved a great international popularity as well. In addition to these (1816), one of his most important successes was the *opera buffa, The Barber of Seville,* composed for the Theater of Rome. In 1822, he undertook a triumphant tour that brought him to Vienna, London, and Paris. He settled here (1825) and composed *William Tell* (1829), the last masterpiece of his repertoire.

♦ MEETING BEETHOVEN
In Vienna, Rossini visited Beethoven, who welcomed him with detachment. Not in the least offended, Rossini set himself to the task of ensuring that the Viennese nobility underwrote the acquisition of a copy of the manuscript of Beethoven's latest opera, the *Missa Solemnis* (above, the original frontispiece).

♦ THE CROWD
The passion for Rossini's music involved all Viennese, of every social class. After a performance of *Zelmira,* a large crowd gathered under Rossini's windows to hail him.

♦ **THE WIFE**
Isabella Colbran, a Spanish soprano, first interpreter of many of Rossini's operas of the Neopolitan period.

♦ **THE ITALIAN COMPANY**
Italian opera, its composers, and its interpreters dominated most of Europe's theater seasons.

♦ **DOMENICO BARBAJA**
Legendary impresario of the Italian theater, in 1822, he became the powerful director of Vienna's Kärtnerthor and Theater an der Wien.

♦ **ROSSINI**
At the request of the crowd, Rossini performed the famous "Largo al Factotum" of *The Barber of Seville,* an opera appreciated even by Beethoven.

♦ **SCHUBERT**
Convinced that the Italian impresario Barbaja favored Italian opera and its composers, Schubert, still waiting to know whether the Imperial Theater would accept his German-language opera, *Alfonso und Estrella,* viewed Rossini's success with annoyance.

♦ **GERMAN OPERA**
During the end of the 1700s and the first decade of the 1800s, German opera suffered from the uncontested dominance of Italian composers and singers. These, spread all over Europe and rooted in particular in the courts of the German states, imposed the forms and language of Italian opera, rendering difficult in every medium the birth of a national German opera. The only example of a German opera with a certain public comparison is the *singspiel,* a genre ennobled by Mozart's *The Magic Flute* (above, in a performance at Milano's La Scala) and by Beethoven's *Fidelio,* but still far from enjoying the consideration and popularity of Italian opera. The need for a national opera was, however, stressed more and more by German writers and musicians and would be affirmed in the Romantic opera *Der Freischütz* (1821) presented by Weber.

BEETHOVEN'S PIANO

Beethoven knew that the piano differed from the harpsichord: the former, with strings to strike, allowed the performer to produce, with various pressure on the key, *loud* or *soft* sounds, while the latter, with strings to pluck, produced the same sound regardless of the pressure applied. Beethoven composed sonatas the total resonant volume was magnified, the contrasts between loud and soft were ever more accentuated, and the intrusions in the most extreme parts of the keyboard (high and low notes) were frequent. To better develop these ideas, therefore, Beethoven needed new pianos that the builders Streicher of Vienna and Erard and Broadwood of London promised to provide him.

♦ **THE ERARD**
In 1804, Beethoven received from Erard the gift of a piano with four pedals. Beethoven particularly used the resonance pedal, which permits the strings to continue vibrating after the pianist has lifted his fingers from the keys.

♦ **THE BROADWOOD**
In 1818, Beethoven received from Broadwood the gift of a grand piano with a sturdier frame, capable of tolerating his very vigorous and violent performing style. On this piano, Beethoven composed *Sonata Op. 106,* called *Hammerklavier.*

♦ **VIENNESE PIANOS**
Beethoven either purchased or received as gifts pianos from the Viennese builders Walter, Streicher, and Graf. Following the composer's advice, the builders, particularly Streicher and Graf, increased the resonance of their pianos: the Graf, owned by Beethoven, had four strings per note rather than the traditional three.

♦ THE STRINGS
The strings were small in diameter and short for the high sounds, but of larger diameter and long for the low sounds. During the first years of the 1800s, the builders tripled the tension of the strings; to achieve this, they began to construct pianos with parts of the case made of iron.

♦ THE KEYBOARD
In 1803, the Austrian builder Streicher expanded the keyboard to six octaves. Until 1803, Beethoven's sonatas for the piano were restricted to five octaves. They subsequently extended further toward the high register; the last five, in particular, extended toward the low one.

♦ BEETHOVEN'S HANDS
They were strong, with short fingers and squared-off bones.

FAMILY LIFE

Beethoven was a creature of habit but also eccentric, solitary but at times irresistibly sociable. Always restless, he changed homes thirty-two times. In addition to his piano, he brought with him a few treasured objects. However, he was unable to forego, even in his most difficult economic periods, the comfort of two domestics. Beethoven willingly welcomed in his home the company of different friends who would alternate through the years, but he vigorously defended his solitude during those hours of the day that he dedicated to composing.

♦ **THE LAST RESIDENCE**
In 1825, Beethoven moved into the *Schwarzspanierhaus* (House of the Black Spaniards), where he died in 1827.

♦ **HIS EATING HABITS**
Beethoven's eating regime was anything but balanced and would end up damaging his health. He was unable to overcome any of his destructive eating habits, such as the two raw eggs each day, accompanied by a few glasses of wine. At breakfast the composer drank a cup of coffee that he prepared himself with maniacal care and following a ritual from which he never deviated. At noon, he often preferred fish, even if his favorite dishes were lasagnas, accompanied by a glass of good wine from the hills of Buda. Above, the outside of one of the many houses in which he lived. Below, a nineteenth-century gravy boat.

♦ **GRILLPARZER AND KANNE**
The former, a young novelist and playwright, the latter, a journalist, they belonged to the circle of cultured and liberal friends with whom Beethoven spent time during the last years of his life.

♦ **THE DOMESTICS**
In spite of his democratic ideas, Beethoven scorned and mistreated the domestics hired to contend with his untidiness.

12. THE LIFE OF BEETHOVEN ♦ *From the end of the second decade of the 1800s to the beginning of the third, Beethoven began a new creative period that coincided with the elaboration of a style that was ever more audacious and incomprehensible to his contemporaries. To this period belong the last piano sonatas and the first* Variations *on one of Dabelli's waltzes. In 1820, he was granted the definitive guardianship of his nephew Karl.* ➤▸

♦ **The Conversation Notebooks**
To converse with Beethoven, by now almost completely deaf, his guests wrote in notebooks. After the composer's death, Schindler would inexplicably burn most of them. Above, one of the remaining notebooks.

♦ **Schindler**
He abandoned the study of law to embark on a musical career; he was the composer's secretary and shadow in the last years of his life.

♦ **The Ear Horns**
Beethoven's deafness worsened in the final years of his life. His homes became filled with strange acoustic devices, invented by Mälzel, already a builder of automatons (robots) and mechanical musical instruments.

♦ **Water**
When he composed, Beethoven had the curious habit of throwing upon himself pails of cold water, convinced that he could refresh his overheated cerebral nerves in this way.

THE *NINTH SYMPHONY*

A decade after having written the previous one, Beethoven composed a new symphony, the ninth. They were difficult years for the composer: debts, intolerance for Austria's reactionary political climate, and artistic solitude. The performance of the *Ninth Symphony* was therefore an unexpected triumph. Arousing the enthusiasm of the Viennese were its sonoric power, its rhythmic and timbric richness, the original chorus based on Schiller's verses in the fourth movement, and finally, its courageous message, included in Schiller's *Ode to Joy,* exalting human brotherhood and therefore foreign to the national government of Austria.

♦ THE EVENING'S PROGRAM
The choice of the program for the exhibition of May 7 was difficult and complex. At first, Beethoven decided upon the performance of the entire *Missa Solemnis* and *Ninth Symphony.* However, the program offended the ecclesiastical authorities, who were scandalized by the idea of an entire Mass being performed in a theater. After negotiations, they arrived at a compromise: the performance of only some parts of the Mass in addition to, obviously, the *Ninth Symphony.* The exhibition was a triumph, and the *Ninth Symphony* roused the enthusiasm of the audience, who interrupted it several times. The police (above) had to intervene in order for the performance to continue. The repeat performance of May 23 was, instead, almost a fiasco and provoked Beethoven's ire, because was unhappy with the meager receipts.

♦ DIRECTOR
Duport, director of the Imperial Theater.

♦ THE PUBLIC
The new and influential bourgeoisie, the principal exponents of

Viennese culture, and the aristocrats closest to Beethoven.

♦ THE PREMIERE
The premiere of the *Ninth Symphony* took place at the Kärntnerthor on May 7, 1824, during a performance that also included some parts of the *Missa Solemnis.*

♦ THE CONDUCTORS
Umlauf, Schuppanzigh, and Beethoven conducted. Umlauf recommended that the orchestra not follow the instructions of Beethoven, by now completely deaf, when he counted time.

13. THE LIFE OF BEETHOVEN ♦ *These were gray years for the composer, interrupted by a few important successes: the revival of* Fidelio *in 1822 and the performance of the* Ninth Symphony *in 1824. He continued, in the meantime, with an ever more audacious musical search that would result in the composition of truly revolutionary works, such as his final quartets of 1826. In 1825, he moved to the House of the Black Spaniards where he received visits from young liberal and progressive intellectuals. A year later, there was a tragic episode in the saga of his nephew when the young Karl attempted to take his own life.* ⫸➔

♦ **THE CHORUS**
The chorus in a symphony is not a completely original composition choice. In fact, it was a frequent element in French Revolution music, with which Beethoven courageously wished to identify himself.

♦ **THE NINTH SYMPHONY**
Planned in 1816, Beethoven worked on it a great deal in the succeeding years, intensifying his efforts between 1822 and 1824. The *Ninth Symphony* (above, frontispiece of the original 1826 edition) is in four movements. The last movement uses a chorus and solo voices based on a few verses of Schiller's *Ode to Joy*. In spite of the seemingly traditional structure, the symphony summarizes all of the innovations of Beethoven's style: great richness in the development, exceptional rhythms and harmonies. The fourth movement, which can be linked to French music of the Revolution, also reveals the ideological content of the *Ninth Symphony,* universal love and brotherhood among men. These were the typical ideals of the Enlightenment with which Beethoven strongly confronted the intolerance of the more reactionary absolutism.

♦ **THE ORCHESTRA**
It was notably larger: 24 violins, 10 violas, 12 contrabasses and cellos, and twice the usual number of wind instruments. The sonoric impact was upsetting to Beethoven's contemporaries.

A NEW GENERATION

While Beethoven was composing his final master-pieces, there sprang up in the German scene a new generation of musicians whose principal exponents were Schubert, Weber, Schumann, and Mendelssohn. They committed themselves to bringing the experience of Romanticism to music. Revolting against the rigid forms of Viennese classicism, they favored, in fact, an almost absolute liberty of composition. In place of a universal equilibrium and symmetry, typical of the symphonies of Haydn and Mozart, they substituted the originality and intimacy of the liederistic genre. Opposing the rationality of the forma-sonata they offered instead magic, the super-natural, and the imagination.

♦ **THE WAYFARER**
The protagonist of a famous *lieder* cycle by Schubert, *Die Winterreise (Winter Journey)*. He was a dear fig-ure in Romanticism because he was the symbol of the wearisome journey of life.

♦ **DIALOGUE IN THE WOODS**
A *lied* by Schumann set in the Middle Ages, a back-ground typical of Romanticism.

♦ **FRANZ SCHUBERT** (1797–1828)
Austrian composer, author of more than a thousand *lieder*, he also wrote sym-phonies and quar-tets. We recall the *Symphony in B Minor,* called *The Unfinished* and the *String Quartet in D Minor* entitled *Death and the Maiden.* At right, an 1825 watercolor.

♦ **ROBERT SCHUMANN** (1810–1856)
He contributed to the affirmation of Romanticism both as a composer and as a music critic. In 1840, he married Clara Wieck (at right, next to him in a print of the period), a pianist of great talent and life companion as well as a sensitive inter-preter of his music.

♦ **THE LIED**
At the piano, an imaginary composer of *lieder* and, behind him, the sleeping singer. The *lied* is the musical genre preferred by the Romantics. It is a song for a solo voice and piano. There are two different types: stanzaic, with only one melody for many stanzas (verses); and nonstanzaic, in which the music accompanies the poetic text without refrains.

♦ **THE ELF-KING**
A *lied* by
Schubert based
on Goethe's text.
It tells of a father
and son who
gallop during a
stormy night.
The elf-king,
an evil being,
accosts them
and snatches
the son from
his father to lead
him to death.

♦ **CARL MARIA
VON WEBER**
(1786–1826)
A child of art,
he dedicated
himself to the
theater and to
music. He had
the distinction
of having
contributed to
the rise of new
timbres, that is,
of having utilized
and combined
sounds belonging
to instruments
often neglected.
An example of
this new timbric
research is his
Freischütz. Above,
Weber in a
portrait.

♦ *FREISCHÜTZ
(THE MARKSMAN)*
A *singspiel* by Carl
Maria von Weber,
considered the
first Romantic
opera because
of its musical
style and for its
unprecedented
themes, that is,
the irrational and
the magical.

♦ **FELIX
MENDELSSOHN
BARTHOLDY**
(1809–1847)
Composer and
orchestra
conductor. His
support of the
new music was
not unconditional:
he maintained
a strong tie
to Viennese
classicism, which
he would reinvest
with Romantic
suggestions.
Above, detail
of a portrait.

THE FINAL WORKS

Beethoven was certainly a revolutionary with respect to the musical style of his contemporaries; however, what appeared to be truly astounding was the absolute newness of his last works even when compared to successive generations of Romantic musicians. Beethoven's final quartets were so innovative, even in their reference to ancient composition practices, that for a long time they would be considered the obscure expression of an aging musician. It is only the twentieth-century composers, by now far removed from the classical experience and committed to surpassing musical Romanticism, who would be able to appreciate fully the value of Beethoven's last quartets.

♦ **THE DIABELLI VARIATIONS**
Beethoven's last important work, for the piano, was the *Diabelli Variations,* begun in 1819 and completed in 1823, commissioned by the publisher Diabelli (above). He had asked a group of famous composers of the time to write a few variations of a waltz written by him. Beethoven had initially refused the offer, judging Diabelli's motive to be excessively banal, but later, ever more pressing economic difficulties had convinced him to accept. Thus he composed thirty-three variations, astounding for their ability to draw infinite musical ideas from a simple and silly theme. In the *Diabelli Variations,* Beethoven often employed counterpoint, as he would also do in his final quartets.

♦ **STRAVINSKY**
The Russian composer (at left, conducting), admired Beethoven's last quartets, which he listened to on records, often with the score in his hands.

♦ **BARTÓK AND HIS STUDENTS**
On the streets of New York on an autumn day in 1942, the Hungarian composer Béla Bartók took a walk with a group of Columbia University students.

♦ **BACH**
In his final quartets, Beethoven also astounded because of his utilization of the ancient composing technique of counterpoint, the legacy of the great Johann Sebastian Bach.

♦ BEETHOVEN'S FINAL QUARTETS Between 1824 and 1826, Beethoven composed his last six quartets. Difficult and for many incomprehensible, they surprised because of the presence of dissonance, or chords that made a disagreeable impression.

♦ BÉLA BARTÓK (1881–1945) Hungarian composer. Popular music scholar, which he merged with the newer contemporary music. In 1939 he moved to the United States, where in 1942 he became a professor at Columbia University.

♦ THE FUNERAL Beethoven's funeral was a moving and grandiose event that demonstrated the exceptional fame of the musician. The same frivolous Viennese that snubbed his music as being too complicated changed their minds in the Church of Alserstrasse. His colleagues, who had enviously made fun of his music from time to time, offered to hold the pall. The Viennese authorities, who had often hindered Beethoven, closed the city's schools as a sign of mourning. A boundless crowd, said to consist of twenty thousand people, accompanied the body to the cemetery of Währing, where an actor recited the commemorative speech written by his friend Grillparzer. In 1888, Beethoven's remains were brought to the Central Cemetery of Vienna, where they rest to this day. Above, an invitation to Beethoven's funeral.

♦ BARTÓK'S QUARTETS Between 1908 and 1939, Bartók composed six quartets that he explicitly linked to Beethoven's final quartets.

14. THE LIFE OF BEETHOVEN ♦ *In December of 1826, Beethoven became ill, first with edema, then with a grave pleurisy. The composer's health worsened in 1827 on account of the terrible condition of his liver. He underwent four operations that did not restore his health. His closest friends attended to him, while colleagues and authorities, upon learning that his illness had worsened, brought him greetings. On March 24, Beethoven lost consciousness, and on March 26, he expired.*

BEETHOVEN'S WORKS

The great consideration that Beethoven accorded his music, which he considered an elevated art rather than mere entertainment, influenced his creative processes, slow and thoughtful, very restricted with respect to Haydn and Mozart, for example. The effort, almost constant, to create original works spurred him to a profound search, to prolonged experimentation, to long periods of reflexion. Often Beethoven would begin a work only to revisit it again after months and sometimes years, that is, until such time as he was convinced in his own unbiased judgment that the new version was superior to the original outlined material. Beethoven also acknowledged the value of his own music and therefore was able to recognize the quality of his compositions. For this reason he attributed an opus number only to those compositions that offered a superior level of musical thought, thereby excluding all the works of his youth, as well as a great part of the ceremonial music that he also wrote in abundance. The first edition of the complete works of Beethoven was edited by the publisher Breitkopf & Härtel of Leipzig between 1862 and 1865. Many works still remained unpublished, and to fill this gap, Breitkopf published in 1957 fourteen supplemental volumes edited by W. Hess. The list of Beethoven's works that has been compiled and is offered here is based upon the Kinsky-Halm catalogue. The initials WoO (*Werk ohne Opuszahl*) indicate those works left unnumbered by the composer.

MUSIC FOR THE PIANO

His works for the piano occupy a prominent position in Beethoven's repertoire, since it is straightaway a territory of courageous research. If, in fact, in the symphony and the quartet genres Beethoven maintained that above all he had to assimilate tradition and understand the achievement of the Viennese masters, in the piano sonatas, rather, the composer demonstrated a precocious willingness to experiment. The first numbered piano work is the series of *Sonatas Op. 2,* dedicated to Haydn and composed between 1793 and 1795. If truth be told, Beethoven had already cemented himself in piano music with his three *Sonatas WoO 47,* with the *Sonatinas WoO 50 and 51,* and with numerous groups of variations. Beethoven's first piano masterpiece is *Op. 7,* composed in Vienna. Defined by the composer himself as "the great," it is imposing for the ampleness of its structure: it is, in fact, among the longest of the thirty-two piano sonatas. One sonata that would assure him greater popularity, *Op. 13,* called *Pathétique,* was written the following year. The success of this sonata was due primarily to the emotional and romantic adagio. Meanwhile, the need to eliminate the traditional form from the sonata grew ever stronger. This is evident in *Op. 26,* in four movements, composed in 1801, then very near the stylistic revolution that Beethoven decided to undertake. Also in 1801 appears *Sonata Op. 27 No. 2,* which has passed into history under title *Moonlight Sonata,* known mostly for its introductory adagio, in which a fluid and continuous melody and a repetitive accompaniment render with efficacy an impending sense of anguish. The movement to the new style, not uncoincidental to the technical development of the piano, is achieved with *Sonata Op. 53,* called *Waldstein.* Written between 1803 and 1804, it presented traditional aspects as well as signs of the new style. New are the treatment of the sonata form, a greater liberty of composition, the timbric inclination to darker sounds, and finally, dynamic contrasts that are ever more accentuated; that is, the frequent recourse to contrasts between the very low and the very high. Still more representative of the "new road" (to use Beethoven's own expression) is *Sonata Op. 57,* called *Appassionata,* composed between 1804 and 1805, also rich in thematic, harmonic, and dynamic contrasts. After three years (1809), Beethoven composes *Op. 78,* dedicated to Therese Brunswick, and *Op. 81,* entitled *Farewell,* dedicated to Archduke Rudolph in remembrance of his leaving Vienna during its Occupation of Napoleon's troops. After the passage of *Op. 90,* written in 1814, a fascinating but also isolated piece in Beethoven's piano repertoire, *Sonata 101* inaugurates the series of final piano sonatas (*Op. 101, Op. 106, Op. 109, Op. 110, Op. 111*). Composed in 1816, *Op. 101* opens the debate about the total structure of the sonata, modifying the traditional order of the movements and anticipating some aspects of what is usually defined as Beethoven's third style, such as the ever more frequent use of the counterpoint technique. Among the final sonatas composed by Beethoven, the most famous is *Op. 106,* called *Hammerklavier,* written between 1817 and 1819, imposing for its length, supreme technical difficulty, richness of contrasts, and also closing with a contrapuntal passage. The last masterpiece of his maturity in piano music are the thirty-three *Diabelli Variations Op. 120,* of the 1819–1823 period, based on a waltz written by the publisher Diabelli.

ORCHESTRAL MUSIC

Until the age of thirty, Beethoven did not wish to approach the symphony, an exacting genre toward which he demonstrated a religious reverence. When in 1799, he finally felt himself ready the result was respectable but quite unexceptional.

Symphony No. 1 in C Major (Op. 21) does not, in fact, diverge very far from the model of Viennese classicism. The same can be said of *No. 2 in D Major (Op. 36),* composed between 1800 and 1802. Dedicated to Prince Lichnowsky, it owes its sole originality to an unprecedented treatment of the wind instruments. While in terms of Beethoven's piano works the passage to the new style is realized through transitional works that combine conservation and innovation, in the symphonic genre the same passage is, in actuality, a leap. The revolutionary *Symphony No. 3 in E Flat Major Op. 55,* entitled *Eroica,* does not find, in fact, premises in *No. 1* as in *No. 2.* The *Eroica* unhinges the traditional forms of the classical Viennese symphony. It is notably longer with respect to any symphony by Haydn or Mozart in expanding above all the development section, rich in thematic, dynamic, and harmonic contrasts. *Symphony No. 4 in B Flat Major Op. 60,* written in 1806, dedicated to Count Opperrsdorf, a noted Viennese music lover and enlightened patron, does not offer characteristics of particular originality; on the contrary, it seems from some of its verses a return to more traditional forms. In 1807, Beethoven began to work simultaneously on two benchmarks of his repertoire, that is, *No. 5 in C Minor Op. 67* and *No. 6 in F Major Op. 68,* entitled *Pastoral.* The *Fifth Symphony* surprises primarily for its capacity, demonstrated by Beethoven, to construct upon a very brief and, for some verses insignificant, rhythmic theme an extraordinary musical cathedral, made up of continuous variations and reelaborations of the brief thematic cell. Endowed with extraordinary energy, it is rich with rhythmic shifts and unexpected modulations, that is, with sudden changes in key. The *Sixth Symphony,* on the other hand, almost invalidating the fight sustained in the *Fifth,* is characterized by a climate of idyllic repose. It is also important to stress the philosophical premises of the *Pastoral:* Beethoven, like Rousseau, viewed nature as the authentic source of truth. After four years, Beethoven returns to the symphonic genre, with *No. 7 Op. 92,* composed during a period of serious emotional difficulties. A rhythmic character is surely the most evident sign of this symphony that Wagner would define as the apotheosis of dance. *No. 8 in F Major Op. 93* is from 1812. Upon presenting it to an English impresario, Beethoven called it the "Little One." It is the only symphony in Beethoven's repertoire to have immediate and notable revision after its first performance. Beethoven's work in the symphonic genre concludes with *No. 9 in D Minor*

Op. 125, essentially composed between 1822 and 1824, although the idea and a few notes actually appear eight years prior. If the genesis of the opera was laborious, the task of dedicating it was even greater. He considered various people, from his friend Ries to Czar Alexander, from London's Philharmonic Society to the King of France. In the end he decided upon Frederick William, King of Prussia. For the orchestra, Beethoven further composed *Wellington's Sieg Op. 91,* written in 1813 and performed December 8 of the same year in a concert organized in Vienna for the benefit of Austrian and Bavarian soldiers who were wounded in the Battle of Hanau.

CHAMBER MUSIC

Beethoven's chamber music restores for us a faithful image of the composer's stylistic evolution. The piano quartets of 1785 (WoO 36) are among Beethoven's first works, and the last quartets follow the *Missa Solemnis* and the *Ninth Symphony,* in addition to the *Diabelli Variations.*

The works of Beethoven's youth demonstrate some interesting starting points but do not veer too far from the tastes of the epoch. The cycle of *trios op. 1* with piano, composed between 1794 and 1795, shows us, rather, a Beethoven already oriented toward an original search that will find its expression primarily in the third trio of the cycle. In it, Beethoven creates an essential and unified work in which there is no empty decoration. Haydn advised Beethoven not to publish this trio, worried about its excessive difficulty; Beethoven was offended, judging it to be the best of the cycle.

In Beethoven's production, occupying certainly a primary place is the last *Piano Trio Op. 97,* called *Archduke,* composed in 1811, but revised in 1815. The trio would become the reference point for all nineteenth-century composers. Even though it retains the four traditional movements, Beethoven modified their arrangement.

There are five string trios with opus numbers, included in two cycles. We pay particular attention to the trio cycle included in *Op. 9,* composed between 1797 and 1798, dedicated to Count Browne. Interesting is Beethoven's work in sonatas for piano and cello, for certain pioneer melodies in which the cello emancipates itself from its traditional role of mere harmonic support. Among the most interesting are *Sonata Op. 5 No. 1* and especially *Op. 69,* composed between 1807 and 1808. It is dedicated to Baron Ignaz von Gleichenstein in gratitude for his role as intermediary in negotiating the contract that assured Beethoven his livelihood from the princes Kinsky and Lobkowitz and Archduke Rudolph. *Op. 47,* called *Kreutzer,* on the other hand, is almost surely the most popular among the numerous sonatas for violin and piano. The most meaningful musical idea of this work is surely in the effort of assigning an equal role to both instruments. Composed between 1802 and 1803, the sonata was originally written for the English virtuoso Bridgewater, who was living in Vienna at the time. However, when the work was published in 1805, the relationship between Bridgewater and Beethoven had soured, and the composer decided to dedicate the sonata to another virtuoso of the violin,

Rudolph Kreutzer. Beethoven's talent in the field of chamber music reached extraordinary levels, especially in the string quartet. A cultured genre, it was the favorite of Haydn and of Viennese classicism in general. *Op. 18* is the first cycle of quartets with an opus number. Commissioned in 1795 by Apponyi, and at first dedicated to his friend Karl Amenda and then to Prince Lobkowitz, these quartets still show indebtedness to the great Viennese masters Haydn and Mozart. Truly innovative, however, are the *Rasoumovsky Quartets Op. 59* composed in 1806. They echo a proximity to masterpieces such as the *Third, Fourth, Fifth,* and *Sixth* symphonies; the *Sonata for Cello and Piano Op. 69;* and the *Waldstein* and *Appassionata* sonatas. In the *Rasoumovsky Quartets* critics point out the correspondence to the chamber music of *Third Symphony.* Between *Op. 59* and the final quartets, Beethoven composes two more, *Op. 74* (1809) and *Op. 95* (1810–1811). Thus we arrive at the two-year period 1824–1826, when Beethoven wrote six quartets, the first three dedicated to Prince Nicolas von Galitzin of Saint Petersburg, musicologist and cellist. The chronological order of the last six quartets is as follows: *Op. 127, Op. 132, Op. 130,* with a respective fugue, *Op. 133, Op. 131,* and *Op. 135.* With these last quartets, Beethoven calls into question the sonata form, abandoning the traditional four movements, creating levels of dissonance that until then were never tolerated, and rejecting the principle of the simple thematic elaboration in favor of variation and of a complex counterpoint composition.

THE CONCERTOS

Ludwig van Beethoven's concerto production is usually divided into two groups. The first consists of, among others, the *Piano Concerto in E Flat Major WoO 4,* composed at Bonn in 1784, and the *Concerto in B Flat Major Op. 19,* composed in 1794, to which can be added two transitional works such as the *Concertos for Piano in C Minor Op. 37,* written in 1800, and the *Triple Concerto for Piano, Violin, and Cello Op. 56.* Belonging to the second group are the *Concerto for Violin in D Major Op. 61* of 1806 and the last two *Concertos for Piano in G Major Op. 58* (1806) and *E Flat Major Op. 73* (1809). These last two represent the most mature and innovative moment of Beethoven's characteristic repertoire. We see in detail: *Op. 61,* dedicated to Franz Clement, violinist and at the time conductor of the orchestra of the Theater an der Wien, is marked by a writing style that is communicative and far removed from any rhythmic or harmonic conflict; *Op. 58,* certainly one of Beethoven's masterpieces, closed the epoch of the eighteenth-century concerto and inaugurated a new one, where the integration of the soloist and the orchestra was shunned, to the detriment of the virtuosic solos so frequent in the concertos of the previous century. *Op. 73,* entitled *Emperor,* composed in 1809 while Napoleon's army marched through Vienna, leads us back to the figure of Napoleon in spite of the fact that Beethoven would acknowledge this concerto only by the title "Grand Concerto." From its obvious martial slant, *Op. 73* dignifies the genre of the military concerto that was so popular in those years.

OVERTURES AND STAGE MUSIC

Beethoven composed eleven overtures. Some of them were composed for the theater, and the rest were for various other occasions, such as ballets or celebrations. Compared to the symphonies, they exhibited few differences, probably due to the fact that they were often destined for a broader audience. The overtures offered an enlargement of the orchestral staff, a slower introduction, and a shorter development. Among the most important overtures are the *Coriolan Overture Op. 62,* composed in 1807, and the *Egmont Overture Op. 84* (1809). Of the stage music composed by Beethoven we remember, in addition to the *Coriolan Overture* and the *Egmont Overture,* *The Ruins of Athens Op. 113* and *King Stephen Op. 117,* both composed in 1811 to celebrate the inauguration of the new theater of Pesth, built according to the wishes of Emperor Francis.

VOCAL MUSIC

Beethoven composed during his career only one opera, *Leonore or Conjugal Love Op. 72,* immediately retitled *Fidelio* by the impresario of the Theater an der Wien. It is a *singspiel* of rather complicated origin and embellished by three different versions. The critics have often reproached Beethoven for not writing effectively for voice, but it is precisely this incapacity that reveals the strength of the *singspiel.* Indeed, the originality of *Fidelio* lies in its quasi-symphonic writing—at various intervals instrumental—of the vocal parts. It is this that separates it from classical opera. In addition, Beethoven demonstrated a constant interest in the *lied,* from the time of his youth in Bonn until 1816, with his last cycle of *lieder An die ferne Geliebt Op. 98.* The poetic text for this last work is by Aloys Jetteles, a medical student and dilettante poet. The six *lieder* demonstrate an extraordinary unity of form, in which each *lied* is autonomous but at the same time strongly tied to the others. The cycle presents an effective equilibrium between word and music, as numerous critics have underscored.

SACRED MUSIC

Beethoven composed an oratorio, *Op. 85 Christ on the Mount of Olives* and two Masses, the first in *C Major Op. 86* and the second in *D Major,* the *Missa Solemnis.* The invitation to compose an oratorio for Holy Week of 1803 came from the director of the Theater an der Wien, Schikaneder. *Op. 85* recounts the agony of Jesus, aware of the suffering that awaits Him. The *Mass in C Major Op. 86* was composed in 1807 at the invitation of Prince Nicholaus II Esterházy, who intended it to be performed in his summer residence at Eisenstadt on the occasion of the Princess's birthday. *Op. 123 in D Major,* called *Missa Solemnis,* was composed in concurrence with the birth of Beethoven's last great masterpieces: the piano sonatas, the *Diabelli Variations,* and the *Ninth Symphony.* They occupied Beethoven for four years, from 1819 to 1823. The occasion was the announcement that Archduke Rudolph, one of Beethoven's principal patrons, on March 9, 1820, would celebrate his appointment to Archbishop of Olmütz, in Moravia. The Mass, which Beethoven considered one of his most successful works, was presented for the first time in Saint Petersburg on April 6, 1824.

INDEX